The Abuse of Language
and
The Language of Abuse

J. Andrew Kirk

Grosvenor House
Publishing Limited

The right of J. Andrew Kirk to be identified as the author of this
work has been asserted in accordance with Section 78
of the Copyright, Designs and Patents Act 1988

The book cover is copyright to Inmagine Corp LLC

This book is published by
Grosvenor House Publishing Ltd
Link House
140 The Broadway, Tolworth, Surrey, KT6 7HT.
www.grosvenorhousepublishing.co.uk

A CIP record for this book
is available from the British Library

Printed and bound in the United Kingdom by
Lightning Source UK Ltd., Milton Keynes

ISBN 978-1-78623-444-5

CONTENTS

PREFACE

Background

In recent years, there has been plenty of evidence to show that a range of words, used in contemporary public debates about political agendas and individual freedoms and rights, are being used in inaccurate and misleading ways. In ordinary discourse on radio, television, in print media, blogs, social media, public speeches and parliamentary debates, words such as tolerance, discrimination, equality, rights, diversity, hate-speech and homophobia are being given idiosyncratic meanings in line with certain ideological commitments.

The outcome is a veritable war of words, in which certain people are investing common terms with personalised meanings. By securing the assumption that their definition is the only one permissible, debate about the underlying issues that the respective word encompasses is stifled. The result is that, whenever the expressions are used, a particular, 'culturally-enforced' or 'politically correct' meaning is automatically taken for granted.

Gaining success in the struggle for a particular interpretation of language means that the need to examine arguments for a different viewpoint is no longer required. When words like tolerant, equal, liberal, radical and progressive are used, everyone is supposed to recognise immediately that what is being spoken about is desirable and the opposite is unwelcome and objectionable. As soon as one categorises another person or viewpoint as discriminatory, fundamentalist, bigoted or homophobic, there is no need to produce evidence or rational arguments to argue a case; the matter is already settled by the very pronouncement of the words.

This abuse or manipulation of language, particularly by sectors who have access to the media, silences proper debate by refusing to listen properly to what another person understands by the terms in question. Increasingly, in our Western cultures, careful consideration of another person's opinion is being eroded by recourse to the facile stereotyping of their assumed position. One sees this in extreme forms in the comments that are made to on-line articles. Moreover, those commenting very often resort to *ad hominem* accusations in which words are banded about as slogans, used with invective, and applied, without evidence or argumentation, to the opponent.

It may be that this refusal to enter into a reasoned discussion, based on acknowledged premises, rational discourse and logical conclusions, arises from a deep insecurity about the merits of one's own position. By accusing another person of being outmoded in their convictions, out of touch, insensitive, superseded or 'living on another planet,' it is assumed that there is no need to engage with their arguments. They are already condemned in the eyes of all those who aspire to be contemporary, enlightened, forward-looking and open-minded. There is, therefore, no need to take the other person's point of view seriously or allow it to challenge what may be nothing more than a series of prejudices shored up by linguistic rhetoric.

In 1968, the philosopher Francis Schaeffer wrote a tract for the times entitled *Escape from Reason*, in which he traced the gradual abandonment, in modern philosophy, the arts and ethics, of a coherent, rational understanding of human life. It would appear that the process has been accelerating since the late 1960s, as evidenced by the subjective, erratic and capricious use of language to which we have alluded. The time has come, in the interests of rescuing rationality, overcoming current forms of linguistic distortion and confronting verbal prejudice, to challenge this abuse of language and thus return important discussions to a considered and civil intellectual debate.

The Project

I begin with an introduction to recent discussion on the use of language, referring to the thinking behind such ideas as linguistic realism, ordinary language philosophy, reference, meaning, private and public language, translation and rules for effective conversation. The purpose of this survey is to demonstrate the crucial nature of language in communication, the consequences when it does not function well and the reasons why it is vital to recuperate a much greater regard for precision in the use of words, terms and phrases. Attention will also be given to the way in which modern means of communication tend to deform or trivialise language. I will also deal with the controversial issue of 'hate-speech' (see below), and plead for a return to a temperate civility in interpersonal discourse.

The main part of the study will explore a group of words that are commonly used in a polemical, propagandistic and random way to promote certain ill-considered ideas in the realm of political and ethical conduct. The words in mind are *(in)tolerance; discrimination; (in)equality; diversity; freedom; rights; fundamentalism; homophobia; progressive; radical and liberal.* Each chapter analyses how one of these words is being used in common parlance, discusses its historical use and recommends a clearer, more precise description and usage.

The project ends with a discussion of how present trends to close down debate by attempting to impose a certain 'ideologically correct' version of language can be reversed. In this way, it is hoped that the project will aid a more open, rigorous and honest discussion of public pronouncements in areas of public policy that remain controversial and highly-charged.

The Purpose

The main aim of the study, then, is to challenge the current, careless and presumptuous use of language in arguments over substantive public matters that are often the prelude to controversial changes to the law.[1] In other words, the intention is to engage in a debate that has had, and undoubtedly will have, practical consequences.

Among other issues is the growing tendency, in some quarters, to label certain language, because some people find it offensive, as hate-speech, with a consequent campaign to have such language outlawed. Such a move is reminiscent of novels that have predicted the autocratic employment of 'thought police,' who are given the function of monitoring all kinds of discourse with a view to eradicating ideas that disturb the views of that sector of society which has proclaimed itself the guardian of all 'acceptable' opinions.

In brief, the study hopes to be able to contribute to the promotion of the freedom of speech and counteract an insidious advance towards increasing censorship. It will argue, therefore, that although the use of 'abusive' language is, itself, an abuse of language, except in very extreme cases, it should be allowed. Insulting and scurrilous language is usually counter-productive, in that it reflects negatively on the mindset of the person or organisation that uses it, exposing their paucity of argument and intellectual inadequacy. In this way, it should be publicly exposed as lacking in any intelligent merit, not suppressed by legal means.

---

[1] The most notable contemporary example has to be the notion of 'equal marriage.' When referred to a permanent, legally-binding arrangement between people of the same gender it is a notable oxymoron, since a practice that differs fundamentally from that which has always defined the word marriage cannot be said to be equal. This is a case where the misuse of the word 'equal' adds an emotive ingredient that appears to overrule the proper meaning of the word. This particular example will be discussed in the chapter on equality as a prominent instance of the misuse of language.

The Structure

The study takes into account scholarly opinion; however, it will not be cast in the form of a scholarly treatise, i.e. the language will be accessible and the references minimal. Even when dealing with some of the more philosophical aspects of the study of language, the book will describe the various concepts and theories using non-technical idioms. In style and format, therefore, it will be pitched at the level of any ordinary reader who is interested in considering the ways in which language is being manipulated for self-interested ends. It is hoped, therefore, that the book will have a wide appeal.

J. Andrew Kirk
August 2018

Questions for reflection

1. To what extent, if at all, do you think that debates on controversial moral and political issues are being manipulated by an imprecise and quirky use of language?
2. Words like bigot and prejudiced are often used of people whose views we do not share. How would you define these in a way that is not itself bigoted and prejudiced?
3. Freedom of speech is a precious commodity, necessary for a society to be open to many different views. In your opinion, are there any limits to what may be said? If so, how would you justify them being banned in law?

CHAPTER 1

The Use of Language

"A way of putting it – not very satisfactory - leaving one with the still intolerable wrestle with words and meanings" (T.S. Eliot)

The gift of language

Human beings are mammals who speak. Language provides the very definition of what it means to be human. People constitute themselves through language. When "I" address someone else as "you," I am conscious of myself in contrast to the person I am addressing.

We use language to communicate. Our thoughts are transmitted in words and sentences to others who, hopefully, will understand our meaning just in the way we intend. Communication happens in other ways as well. Our words are often accompanied by facial expressions and various bodily gestures; hence the reason for desiring to see a person's face whilst engaged in conversation. The volume, intonation and pitch of our voice may convey tenderness, respect, anger or animosity, or a host of other emotions.

Language comes in the form of descriptions, declarations, questions, queries, commands and prohibitions. Its form may be straightforward, or, as in the use of satire, sarcasm and banter, it may need interpreting. In the case of teasing, as often happens with young children, it is open to misinterpretation, just because children tend to take words and phrases at face value.

1

Language is enormously versatile. There are many different ways in which we can express ourselves: for example, through poetry, metaphor, analogy, illustration, innuendo and hyperbole. We use many catchphrases and conventional sayings, whose origin is probably lost in the mists of time. They give vibrancy, colour and a certain depth to language. They are not always easy to render into another language. On one occasion, I remember well, a person who was translating an English-speaker into Spanish at a conference, came to a sudden halt and smiled broadly when confronted with the phrase, "to set the Thames on fire."[2] How do you translate that, if there is no direct counterpart in the other language?

Words and sentences stand for our thoughts. Language, therefore, is bound up with the way we understand, describe and affect the world around us. In order to be able to develop our thinking, we need to be able to expand our vocabulary. This is the work of a lifetime. I am still coming across words I had never heard of before as the answer to crossword clues. Learning an unfamiliar vocabulary is one of the major challenges of mastering a foreign language.

Of course, words in any language are mere signs that stand for objects and concepts. In one way, they are quite arbitrary; dog and cat, for example, (or in Spanish, *perro* and *gato*) employ letters in a random way to denote a particular kind of four-legged animal with fur. Those letters, pronounced in a certain way, refer to distinct objects we have learnt to identify. They are, then, symbolic devices that stand for entities in the external world, or for ideas like justice, compassion, freedom, friendship, which are stored as mental images in the internal world of our mind. In the latter case, their meaning may be less exact and quite often disputed.

---

[2] According to *Brewer's Dictionary of Phrase and Fable* (2009), London, Chambers Harrap Publishers, it probably follows a Latin tag, "he can in no wise set the Tiber on fire." The equivalent in French and German refers to the rivers Seine and the Rhine.

Words by themselves do not convey much. They must be moulded into sentences with the use of verbal forms and probably qualifying adjectives and adverbs. Thus, for example, a conversation with a very young child might begin with one word, "doggy," pointing to an animal of that kind. This could be followed up with, "friendly doggy," and then, "the doggy is called Rupert." 'Friendly' communicates, "you may stroke it." 'Rupert' means one particular dog. So, to give a full account of language, we need to explain the relationships between words in a sentence, within the language itself (e.g. with the use of synonyms) and with the world of people, living creatures and inanimate matter.

Language and the real world

Normally we take for granted that the language we use to talk about our lives or life in general corresponds quite naturally to items that exist independently of our language and mental concepts. Thus, for example, on approaching a set of traffic lights, we can detect with certainty whether the light that is shining is red or green (or, in the case of those who are colour-blind, is at the top or the bottom). Red and green are conventional words used for particular refractions of light; the fact that one appears bright and the other not is due to the objective event that electric power is flowing through one and not the other. Thus, when we say the signal is red, the fact of the matter is that the power to the light at the top is now switched on. Our sentence, therefore, is true, for it depicts the existing state of affairs.

The important factor in what might be called the common sense view of the relationship between language and existence is that, irrespective of the words we use about objects and events in the world, the latter continue to exist separately from our thoughts about them. However, this view is not accepted by everyone. There is a long tradition in philosophical thinking that claims that we can only have access to reality through our linguistic descriptions. Reality is something we create and project onto objects by the way we use language. To say, for example, that a certain flower is a rose may be useful in distinguishing it from a carnation. However, the sentence is fairly banal. To say that it is a beautiful rose with a delicate pink hue and an exquisite scent is to add a description which does not exist in the rose, as such. The important matter about the rose, then, is how it appears to me.

This line of reasoning has led some people to state that we can never discover the reality of the rose as it is in itself; it exists only as I experience it. In this sense, we create, out of our imaginations, the meaning of the rose (or any other object). To be noteworthy, it has to exist for me; a unique being. It may exist, for others, in ways that may be complementary to the way I see it, or in contrast. In other words, the outer world is dependent on our particular sensations, beliefs and opinions. It has no meaning, apart from the significance that we extend to it.

This particular way of describing the relationship between objects external to us and our own internal dispositions is seen most clearly in the sphere of artistic representation. The sea, a thunderstorm, a beautiful girl or handsome man, animals, or street scenes may be depicted in remarkably different styles, using a whole variety of distinct techniques in order to convey their appearance to the painter or musician. Their art is always a matter of interpretation. The world is for me, just as I perceive it.

For the moment, I do not intend to try to adjudicate between these two views of the way in which language is seen to operate. However, we may note that whichever perspective is adopted will make a difference to the discussion about the use and abuse of language, which are the main concerns of this inquiry.

Language and meaning

Roughly at mid-point in the 20th century, philosophical thinking about the relationship between the world and the meaning of language underwent a profound change. For a long time, the meaning of statements was judged by the strict canons of the scientific notions of verification and falsification. If a statement was not open to being verified, or at the least falsified, by repeatable experimental methods based on sound, natural evidence, it was considered to be nonsensical. So any statement that goes beyond a description of a state of affairs that can be demonstrated to be true by controlled observation, using the human senses, is either meaningless or it is a veiled account of some fact that can be checked for accuracy by proven experimental means. A sentence can only be meaningful, according to this theory, if a person knows how to state clearly under what conditions the proposition that it expresses can be declared true or false.

A theory about meaning that is tied to such a rigid form of validation could only make sense of statements about moral values by reducing them to statements about emotional inclinations of desire or preference. So, a claim that it is good to do a housebound neighbour's shopping is, in reality, an affirmation about what makes me feel admirable and content. Religious beliefs are even more dubious. The notion that there is a God who cares about my life and wishes to be involved in it is not an expression that can be confirmed in a way that compels assent by means of empirical demonstration. Thus, statements about God and the unseen world must be interpreted as ways of trying to find life meaningful or attempting to justify certain traits of behaviour.

This account of the way in which language should be used in order to have meaning began to collapse when it was realised that it broke its own standards of meaning. The theory could not be justified on empirical grounds alone. Moreover, it tacitly acknowledged that there are substantial areas of life, ethics and religion, perhaps the most obvious, that do not fit its stringent criteria. Scientific disciplines themselves, as methods of exploring the nature and workings of the material world, depend on making assumptions that cannot be verified by observation and experimentation. One is the notion that "every event has a cause." This belief does not arise as a generalisation from the experience of events having causes. It is, rather, a presupposition that exists prior to our experience that enables the latter to support the claim that, for example, a car engine comes to life because a driver has turned on the ignition.

This line of reasoning has led, generally, to an abandonment of the distinction between statements that are true by definition – such as, "all nieces are female" – and ones that are demonstrated to be true on the basis of well-grounded evidence. There are many other statements that human beings make that fit neither category and yet are part of ordinary, everyday language that makes perfect sense to those who use them. We may, for example, judge that someone has made an inaccurate statement about some fact. This assessment could, presumably, be tested by showing how the person was mistaken in their thought. We may also suspect that the person concerned was deliberately making a false statement, in order to escape from an embarrassing or incriminating set of circumstances. This would be more difficult to prove by recourse to clear factual evidence, because hidden motives come into play. However, the particular situation may show the extreme likelihood that the person was consciously lying, because they felt the need to distort the facts or deny they had happened. Further, we may declare that the person was wrong to dissimulate and, in the case of the perversion of justice, should be punished. These two observations – morally unacceptable and worthy of being penalised – are neither statements of fact nor self-evident truisms; nevertheless, they make perfect sense, being open to rational examination and debate.

The way in which language is used in normal conversation has led to further reflections on its use. Some people, for example, have found it helpful to make a distinction between statements that rely on concepts and those that rely on facts. In the first case, we are referring to statements that, by and large, concern beliefs, opinions, convictions, theories, impressions and judgements. We are dealing, here, with the worlds of religion, ideology, moral value and the arts. Statements about these realities might be in the form of creeds – "we believe in one God, the maker of heaven and earth" – or pronouncements about the future, based on a particular interpretation of history – for example, the true emancipation of human beings can occur only in a communist society in which all people contribute freely to the common good, according to their ability, and are able to draw from the common stock, according to their needs. Conceptual language is needed to make claims about human rights – the phrase, "all human beings are born free and equal in dignity and rights" (Article 1 of the *Universal Declaration of Human Rights*) is clearly not a statement about an existing state of affairs; slavery still exists, and, in many communities, women do not share the same rights as men. Finally, in the case of art critics commenting on concerts, exhibitions of paintings, theatre or television productions or the latest novels, they will make statements that are their own personal opinions. It would be bizarre to say that all their statements were meaningless, for the reader knows perfectly well what they are attempting to convey.

Even the distinction between the language of concepts and that of facts is not rigid. In assessing the treatment that should be given to people with mental disorders, for example, we talk meaningfully about 'evidence-based opinions.' After a period of consultation and assessment, based on interviews, clinical history, professional experience and available treatments, a conclusion is drawn, which, in the last resort, despite the careful use of the evidence accumulated, may lead to an error of judgement.

From these examples, and many more that could be given, we can conclude confidently that language is used in a huge (some would say almost limitless) variety of ways that impart intention and significance. The fact that beliefs, opinions and convictions do not respond easily to a factual analysis in the same way as a statement about the relationship between heart disorders and exercise, does not imply that we are unable to make sense of them or treat them as having dubious value. In reality, the whole of human life depends on convictions about the purpose of life, about worthwhile or valueless aims and pursuits, and about morally commendable and condemnable beliefs and practices.

Language and claims to truth

The meaning of language is tied inescapably to the question of the truth of what is being stated. A common sense view holds that all statements about matters of fact are either true or false. According to this opinion, a sentence is true if it designates an existing state of affairs.

In ordinary life, then, truth refers to a belief or statement about an event or fact that corresponds to or matches the reality to which it refers. We sometimes phrase it by saying, *"it is the case that. . .*this morning, it started raining at exactly nine thirty-four hours." This is a true statement, if, and only if, in fact the first drops of rain fell when the atomic clock registered 0934.

The ability to check out the truth of a claim by seeing how it agrees with a certain set of circumstances is a necessary assumption for any conversation, as in the statement, "sadly my aunt has just been diagnosed with pancreatic cancer." The assertion, to be true, has to correspond to a scan or x-ray that shows a growth in the pancreas region, supported by a confirming clinical examination that it is malignant.

This understanding of truth is applied rigorously in a court of law, where statements purporting to be true (for example, "I was fifty kilometres away from the scene of the robbery, when it took place") have to be supported by incontrovertible evidence before they can be accepted. If the truth of the matter cannot be ascertained (by reliable witnesses or some material proof), there is no way of judging whether the claim may be a mistake, due to poor memory, or a deliberate fabrication, intended to deceive the judge and jury into thinking there was a convincing alibi. Discovering the truth of a matter is paramount in the cases of the miscarriage of justice, when fresh evidence or a reassessment of existing evidence points to errors of fact (or the interpretation of fact) in the case of the first trial.

Although the understanding of truth as conformity to events as they happen – what is, as it is – seems obvious. There is much more to the use of language to communicate than to specify facts that, in principle, can be either substantiated or invalidated. Language is a tool to enable conversation between people to take place. There is a greater depth to the meaning of what is being said than determining its value as a true statement. Such a restricted view of language would consign interpersonal communication to a repetition of trivial information.

What a person utters, taken in its strict linguistic and grammatical sense, as defined by semantic rules, may be different from what they imply. Sometimes we may say of a person, whose conversation we are relaying to a third person, "what A really meant was. . ." Thus, for example, we understand that a person may exaggerate a fact in order to make a point, as in the comment that "B is in debt to the tune of millions of pounds." What we really mean is that B owes a huge amount of money, relative to his ability to pay it off. Language is not always precise. We may have heard that C has just won "a fortune" on the lottery. How much is a fortune? It may be entirely relative to that person's previous financial assets.

So, observation of how language is used in practice has led to the view that language does not determine meaning, but human beings establish meaning by the way in which they use words. Individual words are not necessarily identified with any one strict meaning. They are instruments to be used for a variety of communication strategies. Their meaning is embedded in how they are used in ordinary conversation. The implication of this way of viewing language is that it is capable of being moulded and used creatively, according to circumstances, within human beings thought processes. It is not, on the outside, independent of the ones who speak it. In other words, people, in their daily discourse with others, are not confined by rigid linguistic demarcations and rules which impose themselves "by definition" on the meanings we are permitted to convey.

This view has led to the belief that utterances do not have any truth value. They may be correct or incorrect, according to ordinary or everyday usage; but there is no matter of fact about what a person means, intends or wishes. Language is ultimately self-referential; its meaning is not decided by some independent standard of meaning. There is no separate sphere, outside of conversation itself, which establishes the forms of a pure language.

So, the true meaning of speech is not found in abstract conventions, but it is a matter of the role that it plays in social conduct. For communication to be meaningful, speakers and listeners (writers and readers) need to share the same practices and ways of life. Humans are free to construct meaning as they please, as long as it is capable of being shared with other humans. Interpersonal consensus, rather than an external world, is what determines the truth value of an expression.

As in the case of language and reality, we can see here two distinct views about the way that language operates or should operate. On the one hand, there is the view that the true meaning of sentences is controlled by a world external to language, one which governs the way in which humans construct their thoughts and put them into words. On the other hand, some people believe that humans are autonomous over any presumed external reality and are free to interpret life in ways that do justice to their experience. These views about the relationship between subjective attitudes, an alleged independent world and language, have a considerable bearing on the theme of the abuse of language and the language of abuse, as we will endeavour to demonstrate further on.

Language in context

Another aspect of the debate about the use and meaning of language is the importance of the context in which it is spoken. This has led some linguists to stress the value of highlighting the relevance of what is communicated. This approach is based on the self-evident need to ensure that communication engages an individual's or group's attention. In order to achieve this, it is vital to make as certain as possible that information and ideas communicated are relevant to the hearers' situation.

A second principle shows that relevance is measured not only by what the hearer understands by the communication, but also by the factor of how much effort is required to receive the information or ideas. This requires the speaker (or writer) to be able to engage and maintain the interest of the listener (reader). If the person addressed is not attracted by the subject matter, he or she is likely to 'switch off,' i.e. to allow their minds to wander on to some other interest, whilst still outwardly appearing to listen or, if reading, to shut the book or article through lack of concern about what one is reading. Making the conversation attractive to the conversation partner is largely a matter of making it relevant to their interests and life situation.

Meaning conveyed, therefore, is strongly related to the situation of listeners. They will interpret the communication according to the immediate context in which they find themselves at that moment. Context can include not only external factors, like the time available to enter into a conversation, or the alertness or weariness that a person feels, but also subjective elements, like the kind of relationship that exists between the people in conversation.

Another important factor in communication is the life experience of speakers and listeners. Successful communication is dependent on understanding the situation of the other. People are individuals, each one of whom experiences life in a distinct way. All have their own personal ideas about life in general and about particular events. Consequently, the other person in the conversation may well interpret what we are saying through their own understanding, leaving plenty of room for misunderstanding. As we are not always careful listeners, we have a tendency to jump to conclusions about what the other is saying.

Moreover, because, in certain circumstances we are suspicious, or downright sceptical, of the other's core beliefs or motives, we do not accept their statements at face value. Such is too often the case, unfortunately, when listening to politicians or to those who are trying to sell us something. We tend to filter their utterances through our own preconceptions, which may well include stereotypes and caricatures. Thus, we may well respond to another's speech with the words (or unspoken thought), "you only say *this*, because you believe *that*. . ." But, because we do not share the belief in *that*, we do not accept *this*. If we find some statement particularly challenging, either to our system of beliefs or to our way of life, our natural reaction is probably going to be defensive. So, we respond by finding fault in the statement's assumptions, logic or use of facts. This may well be the first step on the road to reacting with abuse.

Learning a language

Grasping one's mother tongue as a child or picking up a foreign language at school or in later life helps one to understand how language functions. People, in the course of learning another language, often remark that the experience has helped them to understand their own much better. We learn a language initially through sentences that describe what we can observe. In the case of a child, through repetition, it associates certain sounds with objects identified through its senses. In the case of an adult, it gains a new vocabulary by means of discovering the right equivalent words to those in its own language. Such an exercise is much easier in the case of a language backed by comprehensive dictionaries and grammatical resources than in the case of non-written languages. In the latter instance, the language learner has to keep testing tentative translations in the light of success or failure in communication.

It would appear, both from the ability of anyone with enough perseverance to learn a foreign language and from the capacity of a child to understand and use an enormous variety of sentences never encountered before, that human beings possess a specialised and independent language faculty. Children do not so much learn a language as acquire it. Parents, when living abroad, are often astounded by how quickly their children pick up the native language.

The fact that translation is not only possible, but largely capable of conveying the same sense in two different languages seems to confirm the view that there are language universals that share rules common to all languages. Having personally been translated into a variety of different languages (European, African and Asian), I can vouch for the reality of understanding that is made possible. Naturally, the degree of comprehension depends on the competence and skill of the translator. The test of mutual understanding is given in the dialogue that follows on from a speech or teaching session: have I understood the question? More importantly, does the answer match the question?

Undoubtedly, the work of translation is an art. From the experience of trying to read instructions for the use of a tool or appliance that have been translated from another language, it is easy to see that translation is not a matter of mechanically transposing the literal equivalent of words from one language to another. Such was the case in the recent purchase of a telescope for my wife's Christmas present. The language of the instructions used English words, but the combination made little sense. The writer had made a valiant effort to describe the workings of the various parts, but even with a certain amount of ingenuity and guess work, communication was inadequate.

Hence, translators speak of the necessity of discovering 'dynamic equivalents' between languages. They are looking for 'equivalent effects,' meaning that the sentences provoke a similar response. In the case of the telescope, the purchaser is able to make the instrument function as the manufacturer intended. Readers of the text must be able to understand, in their language, the same message that the readers of the text in the original language understood.

The abuse of language

Language is a powerful tool in creating, shaping, modifying or changing social identities, roles in the family and society, human relationships and statuses. In the course of this study, I will be giving a number of examples of how language has been used as a tool, often through repetition and resistance to challenge, to alter ethical values, social and cultural perceptions and lifestyle choices. One such example is the change of meaning generally associated with the word 'partner.'

As most dictionaries of the English language describe the meaning of the word, it was most often associated with business: a partner is 'one who shares with another, especially one associated with others in business' (Cassell Concise English Dictionary); 'a member of a partnership, (being) a contractual relationship between two or more persons carrying on a joint business venture' (Collins Dictionary); 'a person who shares or takes part with another or others, especially in a business firm with shared risks and profits' (The Concise Oxford Dictionary).[3] It has also been used commonly for two people dancing together (as in the common phrase at the beginning of a dance, "take your partners") and for people playing on the same side in a game (e.g. tennis partners in a game of doubles).

---

[3] The equivalent in Spanish would be *socio*.

In recent years, it has come to be associated with two people living together in a supportive, but unmarried, relationship. Although this may now be the most common usage, it has not yet been recognised in some dictionaries. It has become part of the language; a euphemism that has taken the place of cohabitant.

This change in meaning by no means indicates an abuse of the word. Languages change constantly and new generations of people adapt their use of words to fit new circumstances. However, depending on the nature of the change, who initiates it and for what purpose, one may conclude that a word with a perfectly acceptable meaning in one context becomes open to challenge in another. In the case of partner, used of a person in an unofficial relationship, one may suspect that the reason for its current widespread use is the common practice of two people 'moving in together' before contemplating marriage (and sometimes without any intention of being married). In other words, it reflects a massive change in the conduct of interpersonal relationships between two people attracted to each other. Subsequently, it has been used to cover not only heterosexual relationships, but those of the same sex; legally recognised, for example, in 'civil partnerships.'

This is a shift in language that indicates a change to what has now become socially acceptable in many societies. That still does not imply an abuse of language. Further factors would need to be involved in order for it to be categorised as such. In the context of this study, probably the most common abuse of language occurs when people begin to use language in hitherto unrecognised ways in order to alter perceptions of correct or allowable behaviour. This alteration of the previously accepted usage has come to be called 'politically correct speech.'

On the one hand, people campaigning for an end to various forms of discrimination on the grounds of race, gender, age, disability and sexual inclination have argued that discrimination is often nourished and sustained by the use of certain terms (of which, perhaps, 'nigger' is one of the most offensive[4]). Language undoubtedly expresses thought and, more importantly, may shape or even control it. So, if these terms can be generally considered unacceptable, and the people who use them social outcasts, at least half the battle against discrimination has been won.

On the other hand, people who value a wide freedom to use language as they see fit accuse the 'politically correct' of stifling debate, suppressing democratic rights and seeking to hijack language for ideologically pre-determined ends. They object, particularly, to the increasingly common use of the notion of 'hate-speech,' which they say is a singularly ill-defined, catch-all phrase that covers any use of language of which the user of the phrase especially disapproves. The notion has been used as a reason to arrest people speaking in public places about limiting immigration, persuading women outside abortion clinics not to terminate their pregnancy, proclaiming that homosexual acts are contrary to the will of God, or declaring that Islam is a religion that encourages violence and despises democracy.

In other words, the use of politically correct language and the terminology of hate-speech has become a major factor in the cultural wars between opposing, ideologically-driven politics. It raises the moral question of who has the right or authority to determine the appropriate use and misuse of language. It also raises the question of when, and if, language can ever reach the point when it has to be suppressed through the coercion of the law, in the interests of maintaining harmony between different groups in society who profoundly

---

[4] Although etymologically it simply refers to any person with a dark skin: French - *negre*; Spanish – *negro*. Its offence comes from the way that it has commonly been used with racist intent, as in the phrase, *the nigger in the woodpile*, meaning a person who spoils something good.

disagree about major ethical and/or political issues related to identity.

Guidelines for worthwhile conversation

It would be an obvious truism to say that everyone wants to be understood. Being misinterpreted is a common experience for most human beings. We talk about a breakdown in communication, perhaps between a husband and wife, or a worker and her manager, or a child and its parents. It may happen for all sorts of reasons: one member of the conversation, for example, has not expressed himself well, using strange words, or illogical sentences, or the other member has deliberately twisted the meaning of what is being said. Whatever the reason, the result is painful. It can cause frustration, anger and a rift in relationships.

What, then, are the mechanisms that may limit misunderstandings and enable the greatest possible mutual comprehension between people using (ostensibly) the same language? Common sense would dictate that the first principle should be that all parties to a conversation are using words with a sense all can agree to. If some members of the conversation are using words in unusual, personal ways that others either do not recognise or object to, communication will break down. In some cases, the distinctive use of a word triggers a negative reaction that hinders listening. The hearer of the word (or phrase) may instantly categorise, stereotype or pigeon-hole the speaker in such a way that mutually enriching dialogue is impeded.

In recent years, a strategy for enabling the best possible chance of advancing understanding has been put forward, called the 'Theory of Communicative Action.' It offers an analysis of the conditions necessary for interpersonal communication to be governed by the ideal of rational discourse, such as sincerity, truth-telling and rational warrant. They have been given the name 'ideal speech situations.' By following certain rules, people would be able to conduct discussions (especially where they disagree) in a manner most likely to promote understanding of all the issues involved.

The theory is based on an optimistic view of the essential rationality of human thought and action and the ability of language to communicate this interpersonally in an environment either devoid of cultural, religious and ideological presuppositions, or one in which the presuppositions are well known and accounted for. Moreover, it seems to assume that communication can be conducted free from emotional entanglements, such as sensitivities to censure, blame, adverse criticism, condemnation and invective. There is also the problem of the will to deceive or to use language to inflict pain. Finally, there is the obstacle of the way language can be used to dominate others.

All these devices bring us back to the issue of abuse; they hinder an open, fair, accountable mode of communication, based on an acceptance of the equality of all participants. There is no ideal speech situation, for human beings are fatally flawed internally, and therefore tend to use language to further their own interests, irrespective of the threat of communicative disasters. Nevertheless, if there is to be a more humane way of communicating inter-linguistically, the existence of an ideal could be a spur towards achieving that end.

Select bibliography

Bunnin, Nicholas and Tsui-James, E. P., (1996), *The Blackwell Companion to Philosophy*, Oxford, Blackwell

Chapman, Siobhan, (2000), *Philosophy for Linguists: An Introduction*, London, Routledge

Cooper, David, (1996), *World Philosophies: An Historical Introduction*, Oxford, Blackwell

Crary, Alice and Read, Rupert (eds.), (2000), *The New Wittgenstein*, New York, Routledge

Lycan, William G., (2000), *Philosophy of Language: A Contemporary Introduction*, London, Routledge

Nye, Andrea (ed.), (1998), *Philosophy of Language: The Big Questions*, Oxford, Blackwell

Standish, Paul, (1992), *Beyond the Self: Wittgenstein, Heidegger and the limits of language*, Aldershot, Avebury

CHAPTER 2

Tolerance and Intolerance

"Liberty means the right to tell people what they do not want to hear" (George Orwell)

Preliminary remarks

We come to the first of the words whose use in recent years has become confusing. It now appears to mean more or less the opposite of what, historically, it has always indicated. In this chapter, I will attempt to show how the meaning has altered and why the change is having an unfortunate impact on the democratic ideal of freedom of speech in an open society. This meaning is sometimes called 'the new tolerance.' I will also argue that showing intolerance should not be condemned, always and everywhere, as a prejudicial attitude taken to certain actions and patterns of behaviour.

Tolerance is one of those words about which liberal societies have learnt to say 'hurrah'! In a list of values (or virtues) which children are taught to cultivate, it appears near the top. Particularly in multi-ethnic and multicultural communities, where people with distinct beliefs and practices mingle, tolerance of diversity and difference is a good that is highly praised as a necessary foundation for building harmonious relations. However, as we shall see, what tolerance implies is not as straight-forward as might appear on the surface. Too often, it is used casually and carelessly, as a piece of rhetoric, without exploring how and why the attitude gained support in the first place.

The original understanding

In its etymological origin, tolerance signified the ability to endure pressure, pain, bad fortune or injustice. It has also been used in relation to reactions to medicines or certain foods. Thus, we talk about being tolerant (or intolerant) to certain drugs, like penicillin, or to dairy or wheat products.

In civil and political matters, the word has a long history: for example, in 311 A.D. the Roman emperor Galerius issued a general edict of toleration of the Christian faith, thus officially puting an end to the sporadic persecution of Christians that had been authorised by the state since the days of the emperor Nero. However, it began to gain a more general currency around the time of the 16th century Reformation, when the assumption that all citizens of European states would comply with generally accepted religious beliefs and practices began to fall apart.

The initial impetus came from those who refused to submit to the authority of magistrates in matters touching Christian belief and actions. From the early 1520s, groups of people organised themselves in religious communities independent of the various state churches of the time. They came to be known as Anabaptists, as they initiated a second baptism for those who shared their beliefs and joined their fellowships, even though they had been baptised in infancy. They quickly spread throughout Europe. However, they were seen as a threat to the religious and political unity of the kingdoms of the time and were sorely persecuted by both Catholic and Protestant rulers.

Religious non-conformity or dissent was the spur that led, eventually, to the enactment of laws that permitted a freedom of conscience in matters pertaining to religious belief and observance. Initially, this concession was admitted with great reluctance and varying degrees of implementation. In 1598, Henry IV promulgated in France the Edict of Nantes, in which the Protestant Huguenots were given substantial rights in a Catholic nation. They were recognised as more than schismatics and heretics and allowed some civil liberties. Nevertheless, the

Edict was revoked in 1685 by Louis XIV, and the civil rights of Protestants were only restored in France in the 1787 Edict of Versailles.

Just prior to the Reformation, Spanish and Portuguese adventurers began to settle in the 'newly' discovered lands of the Americas. The *conquistadores* subjected the inhabitants to a cruel regime of servitude in the infamous *encomiendas* (landed estates and plantations). Some Catholic missionaries used various coercive means to bring the indigenous populations into the Christian faith. However, another group of missionaries (of whom the most famous was Fray Bartolome de las Casas) protested long and hard against the whole notion of an enforced faith and argued cogently for the absolute right of the *Indios* to resist conversion and, if they so decided, maintain their ancient religious beliefs and customs. In other words, backed by experts in jurisprudence at the University of Salamanca, they advocated respect for the right of the peoples of the Americas to make a free commitment either to stay in their own religion or to become members of the Christian faith. Nevertheless, inconsistently, the same advocates of freedom for the non-Christian peoples of another continent did not extend this freedom to non-Catholics in Europe.

John Milton, in his literary work, *Areopagitica*, called for the liberty of people to argue freely for their beliefs, according to conscience. However, he only extended this right to opposing Protestant groups, not to Jews, Muslims, Catholics or atheists. In 1649, the governors of the new territory of Maryland in North America passed a Toleration Act mandating religious freedom; but only for Trinitarian Christians. John Locke, in his *Letter concerning Toleration*, argued that the suppression of non-conformist religious practices enhanced rather than ended civil unrest, that there existed a God-given, inalienable right to the free exercise of religion and that the state had no duty to intervene in the matter of private conscience. He was one of the first to advocate a formal distinction between the state and religious bodies. However, he did not extend toleration to Catholics, on the grounds that they maintained a political allegiance to the Pope (a foreign power) nor to atheists, because in his opinion they denied any external moral authority and thus destroyed the basis of social order.

The foremost architect of the original concept of tolerance was John Stuart Mill. In his essay *On Liberty*, he argued for a strong policy of non-interference by political authorities in the affairs of ordinary citizens. He saw a danger, in the tyranny of public opinion, of the majority squeezing out the views of minorities. He asked, therefore, for an open society in which a wide variety of mutually excluding beliefs be allowed and debated as a means of promoting a quest for truth and the moral worth of independent human thought. The state's responsibility is not to guide people to accept or enforce certain moral principles, but to maintain a situation of non-violence. Therefore, the only reason for restraining people's liberties against their will is to prevent injury to others.

The twin principles of non-interference and absence of harm have come to influence massively the thinking and practice of societies committed to holding a balance between dissenting voices. The purpose of tolerance, on this understanding, is to support an open exchange of ideas and convictions that hopefully produce a society more able to handle disagreements and conflicts. These principles are considered to be of the essence of a liberal, tolerant community.

The 'old' tolerance

Understanding the term

To tolerate another person's or group's beliefs, opinions and behaviour, means accepting their right to express these as they wish, even though one might thoroughly disapprove. It involves, therefore, a deliberate choice not to forbid, outlaw or hinder their openly declared views, expressed in either speech or writing, or their conduct, even though one might have the power to do so.

It is essential for the definition of tolerance that the beliefs and actions tolerated are ones that the tolerating person considers either mistaken, unhealthy or immoral. The object of toleration might, for example, range from someone's belief in the power of an 'alternative' medicine, even though its alleged healing properties have never been demonstrated, to the denial that the Nazis ever undertook a policy of mass extermination. In the latter, highly controversial case, tolerance is aimed at the right of someone to express an opinion (however ludicrous), as long as it is not a springboard for incitement to violence, or actual violence, against a particular sector of the population.

Tolerance, in this sense, is clearly distinct from approval of the beliefs held. The person or authority that tolerates is not pandering to objectionable ideas in order to curry favour. Nor are they displaying indifference: for example, in the case of the effects of obesity on a person's health, i.e. they are not pretending that being grossly overweight is not a serious matter, both for the person concerned and the public health service that has to deal with the adverse medical conditions caused. Indeed, tolerance (as is shown by its etymology) implies the bearing of pain – a suffering brought on by the need to endure beliefs and actions that cause distress. The pain may be extended to the unease experienced when the desire to prevent disturbing theories and practices is resisted.

Tolerance may be shown either by authorities in power or by individuals. In the former case, it would follow a deliberate political policy to refrain from coercing people into accepting what a government has decided is right and proper or from silencing them by making open disagreement with a particular law into a criminal offence. A case in point would be the recent legislation in a number of countries declaring that people of the same sex may be married. Those who disagree that a government has the moral authority to change the long-established meaning of marriage by dint of a majority in parliament are afraid that government may legislate to prohibit their views being expressed, for example, to children in an educational context. Are governments prepared to tolerate dissenting voices; indeed, even to encourage them? At the time of writing, the jury is still out.

In the latter case, tolerance may be considered a virtue, in that it would signify the lesser of two evils. In some cases, take the example of parents who disapprove strongly of the circle of friends with which their children 'hang out,' it may be wiser to refrain from attempting a heavy-handed discipline or from shouting abuse at their offspring.

The paradoxes of tolerance

Toleration, as described above, does seem to suggest some serious anomalies. Three, in particular, have caused concern.

The 'tolerant' racist

A racist is someone who believes that people belonging to certain races or ethnic groups are inferior to other races in their mental capacities, work ethic or cultural achievements, that they are born to serve superior races, and that it is therefore legitimate to discriminate against them in the context of educational and job opportunities. Racists have internalised a set of stereotypes about other races, which are generalised into attitudes that cover the whole race: for example, that black families are largely dysfunctional, because fathers often abandon them, or that black people are lacking in ambition; generally unfit to succeed in a competitive society.

Whatever the stereotype, a so-called 'tolerant' racist is someone who continues to believe some or all of these conventional views and yet is prepared, by curbing his desire to discriminate against other races, to overlook them in some circumstances. However, the belief that one can simultaneously maintain racist dogmas and be tolerant implies that it is possible to turn irrational prejudices into a moral virtue. A racist is not expected to be tolerant, but to repent of his racist attitude. This is clearly a case where tolerance is not the appropriate response to intolerance.

Tolerating the intolerable

If one holds deep principles that judge some belief or action to be morally repellent, how can it be morally virtuous to tolerate it? This appears to be a contradiction or compromise that calls into question the tolerating person's capacity for consistent moral judgements.

In response to this conundrum, some people have suggested that a useful distinction can be made between ethical reasons for toleration (something is *wrong*, but bearable) and moral reasons for being intolerant (something is *bad*, and therefore should not be allowed). Thus, for example, excessive drinking is wrong but domestic violence is bad. The first inflicts physical and possibly mental damage on the individual; the second causes physical harm to another. Admittedly, this example is a borderline case, as heavy drinking can lead to physical violence committed against another, not least in a domestic situation. The distinction, however, can be made, as drunkenness does not inevitably lead to abuse of another.

Tolerating what is wrong may be justified on the grounds of protecting individual rights, avoiding conflict, upholding someone else's moral independence or clarifying disputed questions of what is, or is not, morally acceptable. At the same time, as we will discuss later, tolerance is not an infinitely expandable attitude. It is not necessarily always a virtue, or intolerance invariably a vice.

Tolerating the intolerant

The practice of tolerating views and practices, which one finds disturbing and potentially dangerous, seems to call for reciprocity. If we follow the ethical principle of 'the golden rule' of treating others as we would wish them to treat us, then, assuming that consistency of attitude and approach creates a virtuous circle, when we disagree sharply in some matter or other, we would expect those we tolerate to be equally open to tolerate us.

What, however, should be our reaction if the mutuality is absent? What if a group's religious or ideological stance means that it curtails severely the right of free speech or assembly in some countries, but demands for itself the same rights when moving abroad? This is certainly the case of some ultra-conservative Muslims, who believe that the practice of non-Muslim faith in an Islamic Republic is an affront to the teaching and traditions of their faith as they understand them. So, they prohibit it. Should such people's freedom to preach such beliefs in an open society be restricted?

It would seem logical that those who wish to deny toler-ance as a well-established norm in a democratic and pluralist society have no grounds for complaint, if their perspective is not tolerated by those who believe it would be hypocritical to tolerate those who deny the norm. And yet, if tolerance is a greater good than intolerance in most circumstances (or, at least, a lesser evil), even those who preach intolerance should be allowed to have their say. Such a policy is based on the (admittedly fragile) assumption that open discussion based on coherent, reasoned principles is the best way of enhancing the common good in societies made up of diverse faiths, political philosophies, customs and lifestyle choices. It seems entirely contradictory and self-defeating to deny freedom of speech to those who would do the same, were they to exercise power. As in the case of those who deny, for ideological reasons, the fact of any historically verified holocaust, the more they are allowed to expound their views, the more absurd they can be proved to be. Nevertheless, as we shall see, there are genuine limits to what should be legitimately tolerated.

Reasons for tolerance

The most far-reaching justification for tolerance of beliefs is the obvious fact that a faith that is coerced ceases, by definition, to be authentic. An imposed conformity simply creates hypocrites, not genuine believers. True convictions are the result of the liberty to think for oneself and to make choices without the interference of others. The reality that many make choices by default, without having considered them deeply, does not invalidate the principle that, as long as they are made voluntarily, they are to be honoured.

In the 17th century situation of fervently held, competing religious views, which resulted in violent struggles for dominance, it was not surprising that scepticism increased. Scepticism is based on the conviction that no one is able to substantiate, in a way that convinces all others, a claim to a monopoly of the truth. It counsels a suspension of judgement over ultimate questions and a refusal to reach unchallengeable conclusions too quickly. Toleration allows space for debate, in which anyone is able to challenge the opinions of others and test their own. It inculcates the virtue of humility, by which one may freely admit one's own fallibility and confront other people's proneness to error. At the same time, tolerance does not imply that truth is unattainable, or that truth claims may be identified as part of a struggle for power. Scepticism is not the same as cynicism.

In society, where some kind of *modus vivendi* is a prerequisite for avoiding aggressive confrontations, tolerance of conflicting ideas has to be a first resort to maintain peace and stability. Public reason presumes that the justification of one set of normative beliefs must, at the same time, be the ground for accepting or rejecting other beliefs. By the same token, it accepts that people with contradictory beliefs also have reasons to hold on to their convictions, just because they consider them convincing. So, tolerance is a consequence of justice; it is the admission that other people's moral views should be accorded respect in recognition of their capacity as human beings to think and act independently and be responsible for their opinions. As a consequence, the parity of their right to participate in public debate should be defended.

The objectives of tolerance

Historically speaking, toleration was the name given to increasing demands that the state's power to intrude into people's convictions and ways of living should be circumscribed. It was the antidote to systematic discrimination against minorities, and therefore proclaimed the rightness of protecting them against dominant groups. Its intention has been to sustain a potentially divisive pluralist society, by limiting extremes of animosity, and laying the ground rules for accommodating conflicting convictions.

Positively, tolerance is necessary, if society is going to welcome the cut and thrust of open debate. It is intended to maintain every sector of society committed to a common exploration of what might be considered the goal and means of human flourishing, where no one's opinion is despised or rejected out of hand. It is a precondition for deploying disagreements as a resource for a better understanding of what makes human society prosper. It is one tool in the struggle to overcome irrational prejudices, to handle conflict non-violently, and to build communities of peace.

The old tolerance does not imply the affirmation of other people's views. It is incompatible with an indifference to what people think and how they act – as expressed in the common phrase, "that is their affair." It can only be applied where people take the trouble to explore others' beliefs and try to understand the motives for their actions. Thus, it thrives on empathy for another person's ideals, whilst reserving the right and responsibility to criticise them.

The 'new' tolerance[5]

In recent years, the way many people perceive tolerance has altered fundamentally. The old tolerance presupposed acts of critical appraisal, in which good reasons were articulated for dissenting from the opinions of others. Today, tolerance often appears to mean a non-judgemental acceptance of other people's beliefs and behaviour. The idea that it is wrong to judge others' clear convictions or lifestyles is commonly expressed as a positive value to be cultivated. Conversely, to argue that other individuals or groups are wrong in what they affirm is taken as the height of narrow-mindedness, sectarianism or bigotry. Tolerance is interpreted as a kind of reluctance to have strong views about the choices that people make. The result is a feeble permissiveness, in which all manner of weird beliefs and extravagant conduct are indulged. However, as we shall observe, this attitude is far from being consistently carried out; indeed, it is the very cause of a new intolerance.

Euphemisms

There are a number of probable reasons for this substantial mutation in the meaning of a term. Interestingly enough, they are openly displayed in the array of euphemisms that current linguistic conventions applaud. There is the idea of *inclusivity*, meaning roughly that 'all have run the race, and therefore all should receive a prize.' Not to commend everyone for simply having joined the race, but award medals to only a few, is to exclude the majority and condemn them to feel a failure. All people, it is said, deserve *respect* for their beliefs, on the grounds that to criticise them in any way demonstrates an

---

[5] For this section, I am indebted to the thinking set out in the following two books: Carson, D.A. (2012), *The Intolerance of Tolerance*, Grand Rapids, MI, Eerdmans and Furedi, Frank (2011), *On Tolerance: A Defence of Moral Independence*, London, Continuum.

insulting disregard for their human integrity. So, tolerance means recognising the legitimacy of *different* identities in the public arena. It is exceedingly common in multi-religious and multicultural Western nations to affirm *diversity*. This is the only way, it is argued, to live in harmony in a *pluralist* society.

So, tolerance has been recast as a personality trait or a psychological disposition to *broad-mindedness* and is pictured as something worthy and beautiful; whilst intolerance is depicted as dishonourable and ugly. It is easy to see how far from one another are the understandings of the old and new tolerance. In former days tolerance was seen to be quite compatible with attitudes of antipathy and contempt towards particular opinions and actions, and disapproval of the people who indulged them. Today, to articulate such a perspective would quite probably be denounced as *hate-speech*, or the distasteful neologism, *assaultive-speech*.

Moral confusion

It would seem that this massive shift in the use of language, so that a socially influential word has come to mean the opposite of its original meaning, is due to prominent cultural factors that have come to dominate moral discourse in the West. The new tolerance is a substitute for engaging seriously with different moral issues. It appears that the problem is that there is no longer any kind of consensus about which fundamental principles should inform society's moral decisions.

Today, the general populace is no longer sure that truth about the meaning of human life is discoverable. So, people are advised to invent their own truth; to do things 'my way.' Girl Guides in England, for example, have recently been required to make a pledge to be "true to myself and develop my beliefs": a beautifully succinct statement of the intense individualism that has pervaded Western culture. The assumption must be that all beliefs have an equal claim to be considered valid, just because someone or some group sustains them. Claims to truth are contemptuously dismissed as no more than weapons in the struggle to gain or maintain power within sectors of the community. The author G.K. Chesterton is alleged to have said that "tolerance is the virtue of a man without convictions." This statement could only apply to the new version; by definition, it could not be true of the old one.

Our present era is one of great uncertainty. To use a rather well-worn cliché, there has been a monumental shaking of the foundations. The result is that, in the words of one philosopher, philosophy can help us to discern that all practices and ideas are social constructs, but it cannot help us to decide which to retain or replace.[6] Truth is that belief we can persuade our peers to let us get away with.[7] Given the extent of evil in the world, it is sobering to think that so many people believe that there are no absolute standards of right and wrong and that, therefore, everyone is their own moral guide and arbiter.

The control of uncertainty

The new tolerance is one way of combating the precariousness of existence in the new millennium. People have become intensely sensitive to and uneasy about acts of judgement aimed towards the choices they make. To hear that others are not necessarily prepared to endorse one's beliefs is destabilising in a world largely devoid of a set of comprehensive, coherent, rationally warranted core beliefs. There is nothing to fall back on. The only recourse seems to be the demand that one has a right not to be offended, but to be affirmed. The building of self-esteem is trumpeted as a crowning virtue. Tolerance of an

[6] Rorty, Richard (1994), 'Feminism, Ideology and Deconstruction: A Pragmatist View,' in Zizek, Slavej (ed.), *Mapping Ideology*, p. 227, London. Verso.
[7] See, Rorty, Richard (1996), 'The Challenge of Relativism' in Niznik, Jozef and Sanders, John T. (ed.), *Debating the State of Philosophy: Habermas, Rorty and Kolakowski*, Westport, Praeger.

individual's home-spun view of life is, therefore, deemed to be a necessary means to ensure that people are confident about their identity, personalities, views and opinions. Anything that undermines a person's self-assurance can be dismissed as intolerance. Self-esteem, apparently, cannot handle criticism.

The giving of offence

When people who speak out about their beliefs are threatened with punishment, because other people are offended, we know that the notion of tolerance has taken a dramatic turn away from its original meaning. According to the logic of those who propose to use legal means to curb free speech, ideas that some people find objectionable are likely to cause them psychological harm. The notion of harm is then used, precisely as J.S. Mill did not intend, to curtail a person's liberty to say what they believe. For Mill, the notion of harm referred to the threat of physical violence against another person or community. In certain circumstances, such as aggressive bullying and victimisation, offensive language should be reprimanded. However, to make such language into a criminal offence, punishable by imprisonment, is a high-handed, illiberal action. To consider it the equivalent of physical injury, as if words themselves have the power to inflict suffering to the body, is a gross over-reaction.[8]

That the new tolerance is quick to restrict open debate in the case of people who express extreme views has been illustrated in a number of cases, where speakers invited to address university audiences have been turned away, sometimes before they can air their views. A case, reported in *The Times* (of London) *Newspaper* on the 9th of November 2013, tells of the reaction by some students to the invitation

---

[8] What has happened to the saying, learnt as a child, "sticks and stones may break my bones, but words can never hurt me"? Or, "the pen is mightier than the sword"? Perhaps the sayings are no longer tolerated!

by Westminster University to Sheikh Haitham al-Haddad to address an audience on its premises. He has, reportedly, condemned homosexuality and told Western nations to act justly towards Hamas, considered by some to be no more than a terrorist organisation. One student is reported as having said: "He may not have preached anything hateful that night, but the fact that he was allowed into the university brokers the question of a lot of what the university stands for." Another student is recorded as having responded by arguing that a "university is supposed to be a place to explore freedom and ideas, and for someone to hold such hateful views to be screened and allowed to come on campus astounds me."

Clearly, these students are articulating, as forcefully as possible, the thinking behind the new tolerance. Obviously neither of these students, despite what they may profess theoretically, believe that a university should be a place that encourages critical thinking. When confronted with views they find completely unacceptable, they are appalled and seek to have them repressed. Another student is said to have stated: "extreme speakers might not say anything offensive when they come to the university, but you (will) find YouTube videos of them speaking about extremist views. . .People take what they say as fact." The test of acceptability is that no one is caused offence. In its response to these criticisms, a spokesperson for the university put the controversy in perspective:

> "We champion respect and diversity and provide our students with a place where freedom of speech within the law, means that they can express their views and challenge ideas in a safe and inclusive environment."

The answer to ideas we find obnoxious is not censorship; it is not to send out 'thought police' to patrol the streets, auditoriums, newspaper columns, television studios, internet blogs and social networking sites. Rather we should take heed of the words of Mao Tse-Tung, even though, in practice, the policy hardly materialised: "letting a hundred flowers blossom and a hundred schools of thought contend is the policy." Then, by rigorous debate, those views that outrageously defy proven facts, deliberately mislead, show incontrovertible ignorance or unjustifiably cause moral indignation can be shown to be defective.

The notion of offence is not a morally coherent idea. It is an individual, subjective reaction to a feeling of displeasure, hurt, grievance, or affront. Whether a person experiences offence is a personal matter; there is no way of judging the force of the claim. Moreover, treating another person's argument purely as an insult may well be a means of evading having to engage with it rationally. It is interesting to note, in many responses to internet blogs, how many people resort to personal defamation in place of calmly engaging with the thought expressed.

Free speech, if it means anything, signifies the liberty to offend. Without it, societies become closed, and the new tolerance becomes the new *in*tolerance. Learning to live in an environment, where one might be contradicted, misinterpreted, disparaged or outraged, is an important means of developing into a mature human being. We should not seek to protect ourselves by declaring certain language inappropriate or certain ideas inexcusable.

Assessment

Whatever the reason for the creeping intolerance represented by the so-called new tolerance, it must be judged a dangerous backward step in the eternal vigilance needed to maintain a society free from the dictations of those who have appointed themselves to be censors of what can, or cannot, be approved and permitted.

Much of the new tolerance is directed towards affirming people's identity. Difference and diversity are trumpeted as self-evident moral virtues, because upholding them allows people to affirm their identity in terms of a group with whom they associate. A little reflection, however, will show that these realities have no particular moral value. It is quite possible that one finds an identity by committing oneself to a cause that proclaims hatred of another group to be a duty – for example, insurgency, anarchism, or animal rights. Or one's identity is linked to a group that is involved in weird religious practices or cultural customs (like the forced marriage of child brides or female genital mutilation) that contradict the inherent dignity of every human being. Group identities, in themselves, have no moral worth. If they are to be justified, they have to be founded on substantial moral principles. Diversity is not a first-order moral good. Differences may need to be challenged and overcome.

Granting an automatic respect or recognition of others' beliefs can have the effect of treating error or prejudice as if they are the equivalent of established knowledge. To argue that everyone is deserving of esteem fails to discern what deserves to be esteemed. Self-esteem appears to be a rather narcissistic probing into one's inner feelings to see, from one day to the next, what kind of health they are in. It has little, if anything, to do with human dignity and worth. These are absolute goods that depend upon some external moral imperative, independent of individual personalities, external assessments by others, emotional feelings, achievements or failures. That is why the notion that every individual, irrespective of any other feature, is a person conceived and born in the image of an absolutely just and compassionate God is such a powerful foundation for claiming certain entitlements.

Individual human dignity is also a powerful reason for allowing people the maximum amount of moral independence that is compatible with other people's freedom to speak and act as they believe to be right. There is evidence of a growing intrusion by political authorities and statutory services into the private lives of citizens. It is as if ordinary people, particularly the less educated and those dependent on welfare, cannot be trusted to make wise choices for themselves and their families. They have to be rescued from making 'wrong choices.' So, the authorities use the language of 'support' for dysfunctional families, so that they may make 'informed' choices; a euphemism for selecting options for their lives that are approved by 'the experts' based on 'scientific evidence.' The freedom to act on the basis of individual preferences is being tested by those who believe they alone know what is best for human flourishing.

The merit of intolerance

So far, I have attempted to show how, and for what reasons, the tolerance of other people's beliefs and practices have come about historically, how tolerance has been traditionally understood and in what ways the concept has undergone an about-turn. The change from the 'old' to the 'new' tolerance is a major reason for considerable confusion in its current use. When the virtue of tolerance is taught to young children, for example, in which of the two senses is it being used? I hope that I have been able to show that critical, far-reaching consequences flow from the way tolerance is understood. It may be a virtue, but it could also be a vice (sauce for the goose is also sauce for the gander).

Tolerance has a high-principled, praiseworthy ring to it. However, there are plenty of incidences in which to counsel tolerance results in increasing wrong-doing. The bland, all-embracing admiration heaped on tolerance may well obscure the significant number of cases where intolerance is required. If, as I have argued, tolerance is not in itself a moral ideal, but a morally dependent concept, to have substance, it requires independent normative grounding in moral absolutes. The right exercise of tolerance or intolerance depends, therefore, on self-contained moral principles being applied to particular circumstances.

The decision to be tolerant or intolerant operates on a sliding scale. There are activities that people indulge in, of which others strongly disapprove, that have to be tolerated: gambling might be a good example. On the one hand, people will argue that institutions, such as the lottery, bring many good consequences to society in the investments made in recreational activities for young people and grants made to numerous charities. On the other hand, gambling usually has damaging side-effects: it easily becomes addictive; it leads to loss of earnings that will surely have a damaging impact on a family's ability to cope financially; it may be conducted in secret, leading to deceit and broken relationships. On the whole, society tolerates gambling, even though it causes a good deal of harm.

There are other acts, which impinge on other people's lives, that should not be tolerated. Genuinely consensual sexual activity, even among relative strangers, is tolerated, even though what consensual means is not always clear; rape, however, is not tolerated under any circumstances. Vigorous interrogation of criminal suspects by the police is tolerated; torture (at least in open, democratic societies) is not (overtly) tolerated. Access to adult sex websites is tolerated; access to websites portraying the sexual abuse of children is not tolerated. The selling of weapons to governments with only a modicum of democratic legitimacy is tolerated; selling them to states with proven human rights abuse is not tolerated.

These examples are all reasonably clear. Societies are still able to distinguish between right and wrong actions. There are also a number of borderline cases, often practices that have a religious or cultural connotation. Some of these are ongoing: should society tolerate a religious adoption agency refusing to place children with same-sex couples? Should society tolerate the complete covering of all facial features, so that the person becomes invisible? Should society tolerate arranged marriages, whilst it does not tolerate forced marriages? These issues, and many others, are still being debated. Decisions taken so far often appear to be contradictory and based on who has the greatest influence on public policy.

Undoubtedly, in many democracies today, there is a struggle going on about who decides on core values and their interpretation: for example, if the protection of life is a fundamental good, why are abortions on demand permitted? Increasingly, it seems, judges are now being required to adjudicate, not just on matters of law, but on issues of fundamental belief and the morality of actions. To whom are (unelected) judges accountable for making decisions based on their personal interpretation (sometimes misinformed) of other people's essential convictions?

Returning to the issue of government intrusion into the individual choices of citizens, do they not have a responsibility to intervene, when it is likely that some lifestyle choices will cause damage to others? Excessive drinking is a case in point. Should governments seek to curb 'binge' drinking by legislating on the minimum price of alcohol? The uncontrolled consumption of alcohol often leads to violence; maiming or murdering another human being. A driver over the limit of the safe intake of alcohol is a real threat to the safety of others. What about people unable to control their eating habits, or refusing to take exercise? They are much more likely to expend the limited resources of a health service than those who maintain a healthy lifestyle. Should their choices be tolerated, when the result is that others are detrimentally affected by the lack of resources to keep some services going?

In the long run, in practice, most people are both tolerant and intolerant. The debate is about where the line is to be drawn. However, in common usage, there is an unreflective connotation to the use of both words. Tolerance is generally seen as a good attitude to adopt, because it is positive and affirming; intolerance is usually viewed as harmful and hurtful, because it is negative and judgemental. I have demonstrated, I hope, that both sentiments may well be superficial. Human beings need to be discerning. In order to know in which circumstances it is right or wrong to be tolerant or intolerant, we need clear moral criteria based on a coherent moral world-view that can be defended rationally as the best explanation for our moral intuitions.

Select bibliography

Carson, D.A., (2012), *The Intolerance of Tolerance*, Grand Rapids, MI, Eerdmans

Crepell, Ingrid, Hardin, Russell and Macedo, Stephen (eds.), (2008), *Toleration on Trial*, Plymouth, Lexington

Forst, Rainer, (2013), *Toleration in Conflict: Past and Present*, Cambridge, CUP

Furedi, Frank, (2011), *On Tolerance: A Defence of Moral Independence*, London, Continuum

Horton, John, article 'Toleration' in Miller, David (ed.), (1991), *The Blackwell Encyclopaedia of Political Thought*, Oxford, Blackwell

Horton, John and Mendis, Susan, (2010), *Aspects of Toleration: Philosophical Studies*, Abingdon, Routledge

King, Preston, (2012/2), *Toleration*, Abingdon, Routledge

McKinnon, Catriona, (2006), *Toleration: A Critical Introduction*, Abingdon: Routledge

McKinnon, Catriona and Castiglione, Dario, (2003), *The Culture of Toleration in Diverse Societies: reasonable Tolerance*, Manchester, Manchester University Press

Mendis, Susan, (2009), *Justifying Toleration: Conceptual and Historical Perspectives*, Cambridge, CUP

Newey, Glen, (2013), *Toleration in Political Conflict*, Cambridge, CUP

Tonder, Lars, (2013), *Tolerance: A Sensorial Orientation to Politics*, Oxford, OUP

CHAPTER 3

Equality and Discrimination

"Linguistic entropy makes it as futile to try to rehabilitate mutilated words as to put toothpaste back in the tube."
(Wallace Matson)

Preliminary remarks

When dealing with the current use of words like equality and discrimination, it is easy to have sympathy with the sentiment expressed above. Unfortunately, they have become slogans in both minor and major ideological skirmishes between people of diverse moral convictions, different political persuasions and distinct social agendas. The two words are used indiscriminately to convey either strong approval or intense condemnation. Equality, like tolerance, is what philosophers sometimes refer to as a 'hurrah' word, and discrimination, like intolerance, a 'boo' word. In a climate where language is used in careless ways, not to convey precision of meaning, but a particular kind of mood, both words have become catchphrases. This makes them easy to manipulate in the interests of the latest ideas for social, political or economic change.

And yet, as the vast literature on the subject amply demonstrates, the meaning and implications of both words have become battlegrounds between opposing theorists and practitioners. Equality admits of many interpretations. The way that it is used often depends upon a person's prior commitment to a particular moral outlook, political philosophy or economic theory. This is not always obvious when the word is thrown around like multi-coloured confetti at a parade. It is an unfortunate illusion to believe that everyone may choose which colour they prefer to toss into the arena, for subtle changes in culture mean that certain colours have come to dominate.

Meanwhile, it is not obvious that discrimination should always be considered a negative concept. To discriminate is not always to act unfairly against the legitimate interests of some people in favour of the concerns of others. Paradoxically, discrimination, in the sense of acting preferentially on behalf of people with special needs in society, is a fundamental part of some egalitarian theories, as we shall see. 'Positive discrimination' is seen by some as an essential part of overcoming adverse circumstances not chosen by the person who suffers them. Moreover, whenever one is called upon to judge between parties in controversial disputes, discrimination is a positive value. Indeed, the primary dictionary definition of the word is 'to distinguish or differentiate between things.' In this sense, to discriminate is to use one's rational faculty in the art of discernment. A jury in a criminal trial, for example, may be called upon to discriminate between the contradictory testimonies of two witnesses in the case.

To attempt to put the toothpaste back in the tube may be a forlorn exercise; it may smack of presumption. Nevertheless, endeavouring to bring a modicum of clarity into the meaning and use of words that are used so frequently and with such power may, hopefully, be a useful exercise. They occur in various declarations and protocols on human rights and in numerous laws, but sadly, often without much precision. The way that they are used can sometimes have immense positive or negative consequences, not always intentional, on people's lives and even on the direction in which a particular society evolves.

The emergence of equality as a virtue

Attempting to present an adequate genealogy of the concept of equality would be a profoundly problematical undertaking. Suffice to say, for our purposes, the truly modern understanding that all humans are to be treated equally began at a time (the early 18th century in Europe and North America) when some philosophers and religious leaders where writing and speaking against gross social injustices perpetrated in the name of authoritarian regimes. Over many years, it became clear that a hierarchical society of privileges for a minority and hardships for the majority could no longer be justified, either by the light of natural reason or by theological principles.

The motivating force for a change of direction came with the realisation that inequalities were largely indefensible. The individual worth of human beings could not be made to depend on birth, rank, property ownership or occupation. *Egalité* became one of the essential watch-words of the French Revolution. It is enshrined in the American Declaration of Independence, which famously asserted that "we hold these truths to be self-evident; that all men are created equal, that they are endowed by their Creator with certain unalienable rights, that among these are life, liberty and the pursuit of happiness."

Rousseau believed that equality was the norm for the 'noble savage', who was, he maintained, ignorant of vice, and therefore incapable of consciously doing evil. Inequalities arose, he believed, at some stage in the process of their development, when they acquired the ability to reason about their circumstances. As people began to compare themselves with one another, those deemed to have the greatest talents became the most admired. They, in turn, exploited the esteem in which they were held; they began to acquire property for themselves and their families. "Inequality", says Rousseau, "was practically non-existent in the state of nature, it derives its force and growth from the development of our faculties and the progress of the human mind, and eventually becomes stable and legitimate through the establishment of property and laws."

Although his account of the origin of inequality is intrinsically unlikely, the desire to gain social and economic advantages for oneself seems to be an almost universally ingrained instinct. Once acquired, benefits are defended tenaciously by means of the sanctions of philosophy, religion, legal systems or, if need be, violence.

David Hume argued that justice for the poor was made necessary by what he calls "confined generosity". Regard for public interest or extensive benevolence was not the first and original motive for the observation of the rules of justice, since if people were endowed with benevolence, there would have been no need to create rules to redress inequalities and protect equality. Departing from equality is, he stated, to rob the poor of more satisfaction than could be gained by giving yet another benefit to the rich.

The self-evidently unjustifiable inequalities engendered by a society divided, as the philosopher Hegel would say, between masters and slaves, has led to a flurry of proposals, plans, projects and programmes to establish a balance of equality throughout societies. In the forefront of these endeavours has been the long struggle to gain equal political and social rights for all citizens and a measure of redistribution of the wealth created by everyone, according to their ability.

Defining equality

The word can cover a number of distinct references. It can mean *sameness*: the quality of being alike, matching, corresponding, or even indistinguishable. It is sometimes used to convey *equivalence*, meaning interchangeability, or *even-handedness* – the imperative to create a fair balance of interests. In a more radical form it stands for *egality*, a systematic attempt to produce an equality of outcomes for every member of society.

The core understanding derives from the presumed nature of human beings. They are said to be equal (the same) in dignity, worth and status by virtue of being human. They are entitled, therefore, to equal respect, consideration and treatment. They are equally significant in a moral sense; no human being is more valuable than any other. In other words, a human being's value is unconditional; it does not depend on the person's character, achievements or virtue, but solely on his or her humanity.

The consequence of this belief translates into certain inviolable entitlements that come automatically with a person's human nature (they are born with them). This means that they are not susceptible to being withdrawn by any authority, whether political or legal. Recognition of this fact has only come about slowly: for example, the right of all to participate on an equal footing in democratic political processes, such as standing for election, voting, making representation to governments, campaigning for political parties and political issues.[9] This is one instance of what is known as formal equality. Another is equality before the law: the right of every person to be treated as innocent until proved guilty, to defend themselves in an open court, to have access to legal processes (such as complaints' courts and arbitration tribunals) in the event of civil disputes, work-related conflicts and judicial reviews. The administration of justice has to be 'blind' in respect of the standing or status of individuals or corporate bodies, to avoid the exercise of an unwarranted influence on the procedures of the courts. At a slight distance from these standard civic equalities stands equality of treatment in regard to heath care, education and the possession of property.

---

[9] The major exception to this right is the withdrawal of voting rights from prisoners, whilst serving their sentences. However, the denial of this alleged right has been challenged by the European Court of Human Rights.

For some interpreters, formal equality is the sum total of the meaning of equality. They consider that, to extend equality to equal consideration in every walk of life or to equal outcomes in the distribution of limited resources, results in an inevitable lessening of personal liberties. This is one of the main areas where the comprehensive meaning of equality is strenuously disputed.

Contested notions of equality

A discussion, difficult to resolve, hovers around the question of whether equality in any form is instrumental (i.e. a means to another end) or non-instrumental (i.e. an end in itself). There are a number of fundamental questions that have to be considered. Should equality be valued conditionally, perhaps to foster solidarity between individuals and communities, or unconditionally, as an inviolable component part of justice as fairness? Does equality of treatment only apply to those who equally merit resources being expended on them? In other words, does equality only apply to people who have proved that they deserve a privileged access to the accumulated common good of society (e.g. because, through no fault of their own, they have become poor), or is equality of consideration, without preconditions, the entitlement of all? Is equality for all just a highly commendable ideal, or is it morally essential? Are the notions of equality and fairness interchangeable? These are all significant questions, which we will look at in more detail below.

Clearly, equality cannot mean *uniformity*, in the sense that everyone will have the same income, or own the same amount of capital, or have the same abilities, or even the same opportunities. The opposite of equality is not difference or variety. Indeed, some of the most forceful promoters of egalitarian principles also advocate diversity in terms of lifestyle choices, the development of innate talents and cultural preferences. In this context, it might be argued that equality of treatment is a necessary part of people's freedom to choose. The redressing of inequalities, engendered by the accident of birth, will give disadvantaged people a greater ability to fulfil their personal ambitions in life.

There is considerable debate between people holding to different political philosophies concerning the extent to which a society can implement equality. Many endorse the notion of equality of opportunity, meaning that people have equal possibilities in terms of attaining coveted positions in society, whether in the job market or in public office. However, this modest ideal is criticised by some, as we shall see, as dysfunctional in practice. Others do not believe it represents the real meaning of equality. They promote equality of outcome as the standard goal: the aim of equality programmes should be to make everyone's quality of life as equal as possible. They argue that justice demands that everyone's well-being is advanced, so that those who start life with serious disadvantages should be given added assets that will enable them to catch up in the race of life.

The difference in opinion between these two sets of people rests largely on whether the concept of equality is a descriptive or prescriptive one. Equality can be gauged using empirical standards of measurement that view such factors as circumstances of birth, health prospects, educational opportunities, natural endowments of intellect, artistic or sporting talents and scientific, mathematical or literary aptitudes. Equality programmes will seek to enhance the advantages and mitigate the disadvantages of a person's life chances; inherent either in their genetic make-up or in the circumstances of their upbringing, or both. Equality can also be a political and social vision, in which it should be a fundamental priority to ensure that all have equal chances to live a life that befits their dignity and worth as a full member of the one human family.

As a minimum starting point, the following principles are generally accepted. Everyone today has equal natural rights.[10] The claim to one's own rights requires a duty of respect to the rights of others. Justice demands that each person's well-being is advanced in a way that is compatible with the just treatment of others' interests. No person or group in society should be sacrificed for some abstract principle of the greater good of all (such as 'the revolution' or a theocratic society). People may only be treated differently if there is some relevant difference. Beyond this minimal agreement, there is much contention. I will now attempt to explore the different understandings of equality in more detail.

Equality of opportunity

This ideal is usually spoken about in the context of employment opportunities. Everyone, with roughly equivalent qualifications and experience, who applies for a paid job, should have the same chance of being selected. There are two main aspects to this objective. The first concerns the procedures adopted to ensure the greatest fairness in considering the attributes of the various candidates. The short-listing panel must eliminate all factors that are irrelevant to the post advertised. In almost every case, this principle will apply to people of different ethnic origins, and, in most cases, to their gender. Marriage status, family commitments and age are also factors that ought not to be considered; indeed, questions eliciting this kind of information are usually omitted from the application form and not explored in interview (although age becomes more apparent at that stage in the selection process).

The opportunity to be chosen for the job should be open to anyone interested, who possesses the requisite qualifications, experience, and abilities. Those with the responsibility of short-listing the applicants for interview should compare the

---

[10] However, human rights itself is a contested reality. I will explore this idea in a subsequent chapter.

potential candidates' qualifications with the various aspects of the profile type of the person required, making the task as objective as possible. During interviews, other factors will come into play, such as the applicant's personality (i.e. how they project themselves visibly, how articulate they are in answering questions, how far they have grasped the nature of the job, how enthusiastic they seem to be about taking on responsibility, etc.). In other words, equality of opportunity in this strict sense means that the competition between people is made as fair as possible, by eliminating all extraneous circumstances from consideration.

The accident of birth

Despite the best efforts of employers who wish to give candidates the fairest of possibilities to attain the position advertised, this interpretation of equality of opportunity is formal; it covers only those elements that can be made legally binding under anti-discrimination law. In real life, there are many other factors which act against a strict equality. Using the analogy of an athletics race, the applicants for a post may line up on the same starting line. However, some will be far better equipped to finish the race in the medal positions than others. They will have superior natural talents, greater training facilities, better coaches, more parental support, additional funding. Translated into life opportunities, some will have an enormous advantage over others: better education, a more stable and encouraging family background, wealthier parents who can afford extra tuition, and so on. Research has shown that the influence of one's home background and social class (in the sense of the occupational grading of the parents) on educational performance is greater than any disparities in the educational levels of different schools. The conclusion is that, when racing abilities are so unevenly (unequally) distributed, lining people up on the same (equal) starting line may not be that significant.

As a consequence, many people believe that the formal, legally binding aspects of equal opportunities are only minimum requirements of what ought to obtain. Prospects clearly depend on certain factors beyond the control of the person interested in the position being advertised. The main one appears to be the accident of birth. Into which family and in what socio-economic circumstance has the person concerned been born? The standard of education open to the person, including the whole school environment, and, in particular, the skill and enthusiasm of the teachers under whom a person learns, will be either an impulse to achievement or a restraint on pupils' ability to acquire the aptitudes that will help them achieve their goals in life.

Is there any way in which particular disadvantages of birth or educational opportunity can be compensated for? Does society have an obligation to provide remedial help? These questions have been answered quite differently, according to the political and moral assumptions that people make. The consequences that follow the accident of birth seem to be almost insurmountable. If a person is born into a dysfunctional family, with limited discipline, encouragement, interest or care and without at least one good role model in the extended family, their life chances will, almost inevitably, be greatly diminished.

How does one compensate for a situation like that? Removal of the child into care – either institutional or with foster parents – may not help much. The child is always likely to carry around resentment at the way in which their natural parents treated them. This is a kind of emotional disability, which is enormously difficult to counteract. In the case of education, schools have specially qualified teachers to facilitate the learning opportunities for pupils with special needs. They can certainly help to overcome some of the disadvantages that stem from the fate of one's birth. However, despite all the wonderful skills they apply to their task, their work can hardly make up for the conscientious assistance that a caring family can provide.

The state may already provide equal access to medical and social care and education. It may wish to go further and try to offer an equal opportunity to live healthily, for example by ensuring, through free school meals, that children have a balanced diet; at least for five days of the week. However, in many societies, committed in theory to an equality of medical resources right across the whole population, mortality rates (the average age at which people die) are still distributed unequally, according to geographical location. The main factors here may be either lifestyle choices in regard to an adequate and balanced diet and sufficient physical exercise, or the economic resources to live in conditions that optimise healthy living. It is a moot point how far state intervention can bring about an equality of opportunity for everyone within the realm of health.

Merit

Equality of opportunity must take into consideration the amount of individual effort that a person puts into gaining the qualifications and other qualities that will give them the best chance of attaining their goals in life. In other words, people, by their own dedication to study and the gaining of experience and personal relationship skills, can be considered to have merited the better opportunity when it comes to competition for jobs. Meritocracy, people will argue, is a fact of life; it is a matter of fairness and efficiency. Employers must have the right to employ the people they consider the most apt for the job. In a market economy, for good or ill, competition is the only way of sorting out who is the most able to do the job. If this is so, then those who say that equality of opportunity is a misnomer, if that phrase is interpreted to mean the same opportunity, are right. On the other hand, if it means non-discriminatory opportunity, then it does have value.

Non-discrimination, logically, should be applied in the case of merit. It would be unjust to discriminate against those who are most worthy of securing a position, by preferential treatment being heavily weighted to disadvantaged groups or individuals. The people discriminated against, in this situation, have done the others no harm, except unintentionally, by being better candidates. The argument applies in the case of applications for places in primary, secondary and tertiary education, where first choices cannot be guaranteed because of severe limits on places available. In tertiary education, some flexibility is appropriate in regard to prior exam grades: for example, in giving a place not necessarily to a person with the highest academic achievements, but someone who, in the opinion of the admission's officer, is most likely to take the greatest advantage of the particular course they have applied for. There may also be fortuitous, individual factors (such as a death in the family) that adversely affect exam results; these should be taken into account.

The equal opportunity 'trilemma'

Some use the phrase the 'trilemma' of equal opportunity. This refers to the three elements that enter into the discussion: the ideal of equal life chances, family background and merit. It is argued that any two of these three can be combined into a viable social policy, but not the three together. For example, enabling all to have an equal (equivalent) chance to fulfil their goals in life by creating, say, job quotas in the public sector for certain categories of disadvantaged people would entail clear discrimination against those who, by good fortune or hard work, were better qualified for the post. Removing obstacles from one group of people may mean imposing them on another.

Equality of opportunity is decidedly not the equivalent of equality of outcome. No one can be held responsible for the fact that some will achieve their dreams and many will fail. It is not possible to guarantee every citizen an equal amount of well-being. What a compassionate society can do, however, is offer unequal resources to those disadvantaged by their unchosen circumstances. This is clearly what happens in regard to medical and remedial resources for disabled people (autistic children, for example). Equal opportunity of access to goods considered essential for a worthwhile life (health care, education and social security) should be a standard aspiration and measure for a civilised society. And yet, because of an inequality in the situation of people's basic needs, perfectly justifiable discrimination will have to take place in order to ensure that all people are guaranteed a certain minimum human standard of living.

Egalitarianism

Those who promote a more extensive understanding of equality, going beyond the rather formal and legalistic interpretation embedded in the idea of equal opportunity, are known as egalitarians. Their social philosophy champions the ideal of an equality of welfare, so that, over a person's lifetime, there should be an equality of access to the common goods held by society as a whole. As all people are of equal worth, great discrepancies in income or capital are an affront to their humanity. Generally speaking, egalitarians believe that a great variation in the current possession of wealth is due to the immoral expropriation of workers' labour that in past generations has been the main source of wealth creation. They advocate, therefore, at the least, a significant redistribution of wealth to each generation. In this way, the chances of individuals attaining an equal quality of life will be enhanced.

According to this argument, a levelling of economic income will enable all to participate more fully in the processes of a democratic society. Indeed, if wealth is divided into hopelessly unequal portions, democracy is a hugely defective ideal. At the same time, just as people have a right to receive an equal share of the surplus value accumulated by society as a whole, so they have equal responsibilities to contribute to the needs of others.

Thus, egalitarians are not satisfied with equal opportunities. The main problem is that it does not correspond to an equality of prospects.

To be radically equal, all babies born on the same day should have the same expectations about how life will treat them. However, once we know to whom and in what circumstances they were born, we can predict, with a reasonable amount of certainty, that some will prosper and others fail. A certain degree of preferential treatment will, therefore, be necessary and justified, in the case of the latter group. The objective of egalitarian policies is not only to equalise financial resources, but to balance the exercise of political power in society. The principle of each person counting as one, and no more than one, has to extend beyond the formal precept of one person, one vote. It should mean that everyone has the confidence to take their part in debates that decide the social policies that affect them. The principle, elaborated a number of centuries ago, stating "that which touches all should be decided by all,"[11] is a basic presupposition of a truly democratic society.

One's view of the egalitarian version of equality will depend largely on one's political philosophy. Orthodox Marxists, presumably, still stick to the ideal of "from everyone according to their ability, to everyone according to their needs." Marx did not base this outcome of a free and generous society on moral ideals; that is, he did not consider that a communist society would be created by the goodwill of the majority. Rather, he believed that a fundamental change in the economic mode of production, in which the surplus value generated by a profitable manufacturing operation would be socially

---

[11] This axiom, known in European legal tradition from at least the 13th century onwards, in its Latin form – *quod omnes tangit, debet ab omnibus approbari* – was made part of Friar Bartolome de las Casas defence of the rights of the indigenous peoples of the Americas in the 16th century against their exploitation by the Spanish *conquistadores*.

owned, would end the division between the owners of capital (accumulated wealth) and those whose labour had created it. The fundamental outcome would be to end human beings' alienation from the fruit of their work, terminate exploitation and thus restore them to their full humanity.

Others, having seen the results of actual communist societies, do not believe that the state can be trusted to take control of all wealth on behalf of the workers. They would, therefore, allow a certain amount of private ownership, if gained without exploitation. However, they would urge, at the least, the establishment of an industrial democratisation, in which all employees of an industry, business or company had equal shares in its assets and the right to be represented democratically on all management committees and boards of directors.

Yet others, attracted by more libertarian views, believe history proves that collectivising wealth does not, in practice, actually benefit the least well-off. The philosopher John Rawls, for example, argued that inequalities are justified, as long as they would mean that everyone's interests would be advanced as a result. Radical egalitarianism ignores certain realities of human existence: basically, that if all were made equal in terms of the economic resources available to them, educational opportunities and family support, some would still succeed in achieving their ambitions and others would not. In terms of temperament, personality traits and natural endowments, people are not the same. To maintain an equality of condition, there would have to be either an excessive and intolerable intervention by the state in the minute details of everyday human affairs, or human nature would have to be profoundly transformed from self-centredness to altruism.

The critique of a thoroughgoing egalitarianism springs from a realism about how humans behave in pursuit of their own self-interests. Nevertheless, there are principles to be derived from the vision of a society of equals. The main one is that society has a responsibility to ensure that everyone has enough of the basic commodities of life, to lift them above a minimally acceptable standard. The criterion is not to attempt to promote an equal standard of living, but to guarantee a sufficient access to all goods that make life a pleasurable experience; for example, adequate, affordable housing, clothing, a nutritious diet, free health care at the point of delivery and an education that both secures a good standard of literacy and numeracy and inculcates those social attributes that allow people to integrate into a civilised society.

Equal treatment

Until now, I have been dealing mainly with equality between individuals. In recent years, the question of equal treatment of identifiable groups by the law has become a source of considerable controversy. What does equality mean, when "the right to freedom of thought, conscience, and religion, and the right to freedom of opinion and expression" is being challenged on the grounds of bigotry, harassment, discrimination and 'hate-speech' against specially recognised classes of people? These rights, in the minds of those who promulgated the *Universal Declaration of Human Rights*, mean that everyone has the freedom "either alone or in community with others and in public or private, to manifest his religion or belief in teaching, practice, worship and observance," and the freedom "to hold opinions without interference..." (*UDHR:* Articles 18 and 19). However, it might be necessary to spell out that in certain circumstances, particularly where there is a clash of beliefs between different groups, a concerted move is being made to curtail these rights and freedoms. Even more contentious is the intervention of the law, in cases where the beliefs are put into practice, and the practices are said to discriminate against other groups.

Notable instances, in recent times, have surrounded issues to do with the beliefs and practices of some Muslims, such as the visual portrayal of Muhammed, the covering of the head and face by women, and the slaughter of animals for human consumption. The matter of coerced marriages is another major concern; it is seen in Western, liberal societies as a serious denial of free choice. Also, the freedom of pro-life campaigners to protest outside abortion clinics by displaying vivid images of the development of embryos as well as when they have been destroyed, is being challenged. However, the most polemical contention has been, and continues to be, the dispute about alleged discrimination against the equal rights of those who identify themselves as homosexuals (including other sexual alternatives to heterosexuality). What is particularly significant about this issue is that people professing a sexual attraction, predominantly for people of the same gender, have constituted themselves into a group, with identifiable group rights.[12]

There are other groups, identified by skin colour, ethnic origin and identity, gender, disability or age who may equate inequality of outcome, in their ability to achieve their goals in life, to pure prejudice on the part of others. They wish to claim some kind of protected status on the grounds of their group characteristics. A classic case is the allegation that the generally below average educational achievements of black children is due to discrimination based on widespread racial stereotyping that leads to meagre expectations of their ability to attain high learning standards. This charge is then further developed into the general, and ill-defined, accusation of institutional racism. The point is not that, in some cases, discrimination along these lines does take place, but that this is often the only explanation allowed. Cultural factors and family background could also be a factor; certainly other minority ethnic groups (in the Western world) – children from Chinese and Indian-background families, for example – are often high academic

---

[12] Different aspects of the contested issue of homosexuality are dealt with in much more detail in Chapter 8.

achievers. In other words, it is too easy to lay the blame for poor outcomes in education on racial, sexual or other forms of group discrimination. Promoters of strict egalitarian principles tend to nurture a culture of victimisation that hides other causes of inequalities that may well be self-inflicted.

Discrimination

Successive governments who try to maintain a strict neutrality between the claims and demands of different groups have a hard time implementing policies which treat all groups fairly. Where the beliefs and practices of one group oppose another's, those who make laws are faced with complex decisions as they try to balance rights and freedoms and support non-discriminatory practices. Part of the problem is that, as in the case of equality, discrimination has become a 'mutilated word'. It is often used as a kind of trump card to bring a reasoned argument to a summary end.

So, in the conflict of interests that prevail in any open society, where the honest exchange of different, passionately-held views is still encouraged, the language of discrimination is often marshalled to evade intricate questions. For example, if the beliefs and/or practices of a particular group of people, be they religious or non-religious, are challenged, the holders of the beliefs may instantly complain that they are being discriminated against. The assumption behind the complaint is that equality of respect for people implies equality of respect for their beliefs and practices, simply because their beliefs are said to form an essential part of their primary identity. If no distinction is made between the content of a belief and the person holding it, all criticisms of beliefs are, logically, a censure of the person.

However, a moment's thought shows that this interpretation of discrimination is false. Not all beliefs are equally valid. Beliefs that contradict others cannot all be true. Some beliefs must be judged acceptable and others inadmissible. In the last analysis, a society does not and should not respect all beliefs equally. Notwithstanding, a person's intrinsic value as a human being does not depend on the content of the beliefs they may espouse. Even people who have committed great evils, motivated by their extremely depraved creeds or ideologies, are still humans.

That being said, a society aspiring to be open and democratic will be judged largely on its ability to facilitate a reasoned debate about differences of opinion. A reasoned debate is one that takes other people's views at face value and tries to understand the grounds on which they are based, the mode of argument used to justify them, the motive(s) for promoting them, and the intention in putting them forward. A reasoned debate refrains from ascribing dishonourable motives to those with whom we disagree by making sweeping accusations of prejudice, sectarianism or fanaticism. A reasoned debate shuns all attempts at personal character assassination; however subtle and well-camouflaged they may appear to be. It does not rule out of order beliefs that are based on non-empirical grounds; moral convictions, for example, can rarely, if ever, be defended purely on the basis of what is the case. No authentically-held belief has an automatic veto on other beliefs, nor does any group have an *a priori* right to silence others, by claiming that it is being disrespected or victimised.

Unfortunately, our contemporary, liberal societies are losing the ability to reason openly, civilly and intelligently. Too often, discourse about equality and discrimination is conducted with the use of rhetoric, slogans, false claims, defamations, unfounded allegations and systematic misrepresentations. A prime example of this has been the dispute about the contro-versial term, 'equal marriage.'

Equal marriage?

It is not my intention, in this chapter, to deal with the whole thorny issue of homosexual orientation and the rights that are said to follow from such a situation, nor the use of the language of 'homophobia' to characterise those who do not accept the homosexual agenda. I will explore the use of this language and what it implies in a later chapter. The intention here is more modest: to examine and evaluate the question of whether the civil union of two people of the same sex can be qualified by the epithet 'equal' in the context of the long-standing institution of heterosexual marriage.[13] I will attempt to do this by looking at possible meanings of the word equal and judging whether any of them fit the context of marriage, in its time-honoured meaning, of the 'legal union made by a man and a woman to live together as husband and wife.' In other words, is the language of equality being legitimately extended to the alliance formed by two people of the same sex, or is it being used in a novel and idiosyncratic way?

As we have already explored, equal can have a range of meanings. For our purposes in this debate, we look at the following: *identical, equivalent, corresponding,* and *even-handedness*. Can any of these words justifiably be made to apply when the two sets of relationship (heterosexual and homosexual) are compared? Well, clearly the two arrangements are not *identical*. There are significant differences in the ways in which people of the same sex and the opposite sex bond. Two men or two women can form very deep friendships, but the element of gender complementarity is, by definition, absent. Also, by biological differentiation, the procreation of children by virtue of a sexual union between the two is also absent. In a heterosexual marriage, the consummation will normally, sooner or later, issue in the birth of the next generation of human beings. The addition to the family is the result of the mutual decision of husband and wife to care for and nurture the fruit of their specific union. There are obvious

---

[13] In a later chapter, I will also look at other arguments, besides those based on the notion of equality, in favour of same-sex marriage.

exceptions to this general rule: when people marry beyond child-bearing age, or when the couple are unable to have children or decide not to. However, these are special cases, representing a minority of marriages. Homosexual partnerships may bring up children; the offspring of one partner and an outside agent, or through adoption. In neither case will the child be the direct result of their specific union. For these reasons, the marriages are decidedly not *identical*.

Are the set-ups *equivalent*? Defenders of equal rights in the instance of marriage claim, on the grounds of equal commitment, that there is an equivalence of status between heterosexual marriage and gay partnership. Equivalent is usually taken to mean that two entities are interchangeable; that in each case, we are talking of the same basic category. However, in the instance of marriage, this is clearly not the case. The kind of bonds that are developed between people of the same and opposite sex are of a different order. Gender cannot be obliterated, as if it were irrelevant to relationships.

Moreover, numerous studies have shown that children flourish best in an environment where there is a mother and a father in a long-lasting, dedicated relationship, which is sanctioned by the public ceremony of marriage. This is not to deny that there are other forms of family, but to affirm that they are dissimilar and, from the children's perspective, less than ideal. One presumes, for example, that the case of a mother or father bringing up a child on their own is not what either would consider ideal,[14] even when there may be good grounds for divorce or separation. The presence of the father and the mother is necessary for the child to be able to see how, in practice, a desirable relationship between people of the opposite sex is to be modelled. A same-sex partnership cannot create a family where children will know and relate to both a

---

[14] The frequent remarriage of a father or mother in these circumstances, or in the case of one or the other having died, seems to bear out this assumption.

father and a mother. So, the argument from equality, derived from the notion that the two forms of marriage are *equivalent*, breaks down.

Do these two different kinds of union in some way *correspond*? Those who support 'equal marriage' argue that, in the same way as heterosexual marriage, it expresses a faithful covenant between two people deeply in love. Therefore, it is intolerable to deny same sex couples a similar institution and status. However, again, a little thought will show that the commitments do not *correspond*. In the case of heterosexual marriage, the commitment is to someone who one hopes (in most cases) will be either father or mother to the children they will jointly bring to birth and nurture. This, surely, must be a factor in the choice of a life-long partner. The commitment is also to someone who is equal, but sexually different, and who, therefore, genuinely complements the other. The latter would be the main argument for distinguishing between a marriage that does not issue in offspring and a same-sex relationship. Complementarity is, by definition, absent from a partnership of two people of the same gender.

Homosexual marriages possess their own linguistic difficulties: how does one speak of husband and wife or, where children are present, father and mother? In the first case, people may use the word partner. However, this word is used in other circumstances, where marriage has not been entered into. In the second case, some people use the terms 'parent one' and 'parent two'. However, such an artificial means of escaping from the linguistic confusion created by the idea of equal marriage, the notion of equality, is damaged by the notion of one and two; even the use of 'parent A' and 'parent B' gives a flavour of their being a hierarchy in the relationship.

We come to the final argument in favour of 'equal marriage': that the issue is equivalent to the case of equal rights and entitlements between men and women and for people of every race. If this were so, equality as *even-handedness* would have to be applied; to the contrary, society would be guilty of a blatant inconsistency and unjustifiable discrimination. However, if homosexuality were to be considered the equivalent of gender or race in terms of equal rights (or, for that matter, disability or age), it would have to be true that a sexual preference for the same sex (homosexuality) is inherent in one's nature from conception. So far, no one has been able to substantiate this claim based on the same kind of incontrovertible evidence that exists in the case of gender, race, age or disability. It has been pointed out that, unlike race and gender, homosexual relations are expressed through behaviour, not in identifiable physical attributes; otherwise, the action of 'coming out' would be unnecessary.

Homosexual identity, therefore, is manifest only in conduct. To declare oneself homosexual, therefore, is a personal conviction, which can be acted on in different ways. It is not comparable to skin colour or gender, which are permanent physiological features. The question then becomes, why is this particular group accorded special treatment for the beliefs it holds, whilst those who oppose these beliefs on the grounds that they hold different convictions are accorded lesser freedoms and rights? Why do self-proclaimed homosexuals receive more protection from the law, on the grounds of their beliefs, than those who dispute them, due to other beliefs? Is it not the case, therefore, that law-makers in Parliament, who promulgate the law, are not acting impartially and *even-handedly*, but taking sides?

As none of the possible synonyms for *equal* fit the category of same-sex marriage, when compared with the customary definition, we are bound to conclude that the case for *equal* marriage has not been made. It is often said that if people are treated differently, it must be on the basis that there are relevant differences between them. This is exactly true in this case; the differences are conspicuous. Therefore, the claim that a denial of equal rights in this instance is explicit discrimination against equality is based on a clear confusion of categories. The term 'equal marriage' is an oxymoron. It is a figment of the imagination. What does not exist in the real world cannot be sensibly spoken about.[15] It is an abuse of language.

The basis for equality

Equality, along with the language of rights, "is becoming the supreme value of our political and legal discourse, yet its nature and requirements remain remarkably elusive."[16] Both these affirmations are statements of the obvious. However, to announce what is manifest does not necessarily help us to sort out the many ambiguities and anomalies in the use and abuse of the word.

It might help to gain greater clarification if the principal premise that all people are born equal were to be given a credible foundation. The empirical reality is the reverse: people are born in quite unequal circumstances and, with few exceptions, have to bear the consequences of their birth situation throughout their lives. How, then, do contemporary societies that proclaim the supreme virtue of equality justify their stance?

Within the context of the predominantly secular outlook on life characteristic of most liberal societies, many attempts have been made. The secular account is based on at least a couple of basic premises: that it is neutral between competing religious views, and that it is the only account supported by evidence and reason. Moreover, it is alleged that the only firm evidence (empirically demonstrable) for the origin of humankind is the one given in a modified version of Darwin's *Origin of Species*, namely *that all life* has come about by a chance evolutionary process of mutation and adaptation.

---

[15] The discussion may remind one of Wittgenstein's immortal words: "A nothing would serve just as well as a something about which nothing could be said," *Philosophical Investigations(1953)*, Oxford, Blackwell #304.

[16] Rivers, Julian, (2006), 'The Abuse of Equality', *Ethics in Brief*, Summer, Vol. 11, No. 1.

This being so, the range and nature of human characteristics are equally the result of chance. That there is no independent measure of the worth of human beings is the logical conclusion of the secular outlook.

Given this as a presuppositional background, a number of attempts have been made to ground equality in something other than purely subjective and/or emotive reasoning. As clearly all human beings have many similar capacities – among others, to feel joy and pain, to reason, to absorb knowledge, to make decisions, to create priorities and plan for the future, to distinguish between good and evil, attributes that separate them from other mammals – there should be a presumption towards treating people equally. Then there is the case that most people would subscribe to the general ('golden') rule that they should treat others as they wish to be treated. Logically, if they do not accord others equality of status, they cannot expect to be so treated themselves; but then their moral values would be incoherent.

A variant of this argument is the (Kantian) axiom that all people should be treated as ends in themselves, never as a means to another person's end. Again, this is precisely what they would wish for themselves. Another strategy that some use is to affirm that treating people equally has served society well. Society functions at its optimum when all are treated fairly. There are good consequential grounds, therefore, for affirming people's basic equality. Yet others base human equality on the libertarian principle that all are born free, and therefore their free will should not be coerced by arbitrary power. No one can claim a greater right to freedom of belief, conscience, association, speech and respect than anyone else. These fundamental freedoms are to be implemented equally for every citizen without distinction. Finally, some claim that their commitment to equality is simply a basic belief. Therefore, it does not need to be justified. Intuitively, we know that we belong to the same species, and that our sameness far outweighs inherited or culturally-determined differences.

There are two basic problems with all these attempts to ground concepts of equal dignity or worth in principles acceptable to a secular (or naturalistic) mindset. Firstly, they all focus on some attribute or another that human beings are said to possess – reason, moral discernment, freedom, or whatever. They can give no account of why beings that, for various causes, do not possess these, or only possess them in very limited supplies, should be considered equal. What human value do we place on a human embryo, a severely brain-damaged child, an autistic person, a psychopath, an old person with advanced dementia or even someone, mentally alert, who has been convicted of extreme cruelty and refuses to acknowledge wrong? In these cases, limited maybe, but nevertheless real, a number of attributes that qualify them to be called human are missing. Do they, therefore, have a lesser human status? Some would say yes: it is counter-intuitive to equate an imbecile with, say, a professor of mathematics in the prime of his career; because their personalities function in radically different ways, they cannot be accorded the same worth.

Secondly, the naturalistic account of the origin of the human species, as we know it today, gives no coherent account as to why all those who have somehow survived the random process of natural selection should be considered equal. If the reality is that we have survived because we are the fittest, and if survival and the replenishing of the gene pool is all that nature requires, then why would we bother to intervene to eliminate chronic diseases that kill thousands each year, or spend huge amounts of money trying to save the lives of vulnerable babies through intensive, intrusive surgery and post-operational care? Why would it be wrong to practise eugenics: the selection of mates with the best chance of producing the physically and mentally strongest specimens, eliminating weak links from the genealogical chain? Why do eugenics and euthanasia summon distaste, if not horror, into most peoples' consciences? Should they not be logical outcomes of a naturalistic account of human origins?

If all these attempts to ground equal dignity, moral value or worth in something more substantial than a description of human beings fail, as they are bound to, is anything left? Is there an adequate alternative foundation for according all human beings total, equal status that does not depend on their qualities, the circumstances of their birth or their position in society? The obvious answer would seem to be that the guarantor of equal, intrinsic and inalienable human dignity and honour has to come from outside the human species altogether. This would appear to be the only way of establishing a wholly independent moral source; one that can be appealed to as having an entirely impartial existence and representing an absolute standpoint.

This was certainly the view of those who, from at least the late Middle Ages, began to speak in earnest about human rights. The only reality that appears to fit the description is a personal divine being who has created every person individually in the same divine image, conferring on each an equal consideration. The notion of *being created* equal removes the necessity of attempting to find reasons for observing equal rights and obligations wholly *from within* a secular and naturalistic world-view. Ideas such as human dignity and the sanctity of life have no adequate backing unless there is an unassailable justification that works independently of human reason alone. Such ideas could just as easily be useful fictions, designed to counteract the human propensity to promote their own ends; if necessary, with the use of a superior force. Belief in creation is further supported by belief that the creator, without any exception, also cares equally and specially for every human. According to this argument, equality cannot be an ultimate moral value, for it depends on a reality more ultimate and presupposes it:

"The originators of rights language presupposed a theistic world-view, and secular advocates of equal rights are, to cite Tolstoy, like children who see beautiful flowers, grab them, break them at their stems, and try to transplant them without their roots."[17]

So, the God factor gives both necessary and sufficient grounds for the flourishing of the roots. The image of God in the human is a non-natural property (a relationship of grace, not an inherited characteristic or reward for some achievement). The naturalist argument is foreclosed, since not every human being possesses the same empirical qualities. The inadequacy of the naturalist attempt to find an adequate ground for recognising the equal moral status of every person born into the world does not mean that a god exists. However, even if God does not exist, there is an excellent reason (in this case) to invent him. Nevertheless, it would be entirely unsatisfactory to found such an important belief as equal moral worth on a fabrication. Is there any other alternative than the choice between a naturalist account of moral values and divine disclosure? A convincing answer is still awaited. Meanwhile, to use another metaphor, it appears nonsensical to blow up bridges and still hope to drive vehicles across them.

Conclusion

In contemporary late modern societies, there is an ongoing debate between egalitarians and libertarians about the relative merits of equality and liberty. Where the two seem to clash, the right approach to judging their respective merits would seem to be to treat each instance as a separate case. For example, if laws are enacted to try to banish pornography from being openly accessible on the internet, some will say that this is a limitation on the freedom of adults to indulge

---

[17] Pojman, Louis (1997), 'On Equal Human Worth: A Critique of Contemporary Egalitarianism', in Pojman, Louis and Westmoreland, Robert (eds.), *Equality: Selected Readings*, Oxford, OUP p. 295.

their sexual fantasies as they wish. Others, however, will argue that the move helps to promote equal opportunities for women, on the basis that pornography damages the image of women by implying that their main value is as sex objects. It is a stereotypical representation that belittles their real worth. Moreover, as women deserve to be liberated from all degrading images of their physicality, freedom is also being promoted in this case. (Pornography can be regarded as an expressive symptom of a return to barbarism: a loss of civility and civilisation).

Arguments from equality cannot be made to trump the basic human freedom of speech. There appears to be a strong conviction, in certain circles, that only some beliefs are admissible in open, public debate. For example, some secularists will argue that proposals affecting issues of equality and discrimination can only be promoted on grounds that most, if not all, other citizens can reasonably accept. This is then said to rule out reasons that are based on religious convictions, seeing that religious beliefs are now only held by a minority of the population of Western societies and, in any case, they tend to contradict one another. Thus, discussions about what constitutes equality, and in what circumstances it ought to be practised, should only be engaged with on the basis of non-religious standpoints.

Such a stance actually denies not only basic liberties, but also equality of treatment. It represents the opposite of an open society, in which people are free to state the most outrageous views, including the idea that equality is a myth dreamed up to further the interests of those who fail to succeed in fulfilling their life ambitions. A society that feels threatened by the free exchange of convictions, in which all citizens have an equal opportunity to express themselves without fear of censure, can hardly be said to be a robust democratic community. Its advocacy of equality becomes hypocritical; its championing of liberty even more so.

I believe that I have given enough evidence and produced enough arguments to show that a simple, unsophisticated use of the concept of equality to make a point, conclude an argument or justify changes to the law is to abuse language. Equality has a number of different meanings. Unfortunately, it is often used to convey contradictory notions. It is regularly used incorrectly, more to convey a mood, perception or passion than to advance a reasoned discussion based on carefully defined meanings. The intention of this chapter has been to uphold the important value of equality in its many dimensions, whilst criticising the numerous misrepresentations that are current in public debate, as well as national and international policies. The reader will judge whether I have succeeded in putting just a little toothpaste back in the tube.

Select bibliography

Cavanagh, Matt, (2002), *Against Equality of Opportunity*, Oxford, OUP

Christiano, Thomas, (2008), *The Constitution of Equality: Democratic Authority and its Limits*, Oxford, OUP

Clayton, Matthew and Williams, Andrew (eds.), (2002), *The Ideal of Equality*, Basingstoke, Macmillan

Kagan, Shelly, (2012), *The Geometry of Desert*, Oxford, OUP

Phillips, Anne, (2004), 'Defending Equality of Outcome,' *Journal of Political Philosophy*, pp. 1-19

Pojman, Louis P. and Westmoreland, Robert (eds.), (1997), *Equality: Selected Readings*, Oxford, OUP

Rawls, John, *Justice as Fairness: A Restatement* (Erin Kelly, ed.), (2005), Cambridge, MA, Harvard University Press

Roemer, John, (1998), *Equality of Opportunity,* Cambridge: CUP

Saunders, Peter, (2011), *The Rise of the Equality Industry*, London, Civitas

Thompson, Neil, (2011/3), *Promoting Equality: Working with Diversity and Difference,* Basingstoke, Palgrave Macmillan

CHAPTER 4

Freedom and Choice

"It is by the goodness of God that in our country we have those three unspeakably precious things: freedom of speech, freedom of conscience, and the prudence never to practise either of them." (Mark Twain, *Following the Equator*)

Preliminary remarks

The enjoyment of an expanding range of freedoms is one of the most prized of human possessions. People all over the globe have, to coin a phrase, 'fallen in love' with freedom. Those who live under the rule of brutal and corrupt regimes wish to be able to determine their own future. Those who live in the degrading conditions of urban or rural poverty long to be free of the cycle of deprivation in which they are trapped. Women, experiencing domestic violence, seek ways to free themselves from the inhuman treatment they are forced to suffer. Young people crave to break free from the fussy and critical attention they receive from their parents. The directors and managers of industry and businesses battle to be free from legislation that inhibits their economic freedoms. Trade Unions struggle to free their members from the imposition of adverse working practices and exploitative wages. Many see the pursuit of the greatest possible freedom of choice in education, jobs, leisure activities, satisfying personal relationships, medical care and financial security for retirement, as a sufficient purpose in life. Simply put, they wish to be able, ideally at all times, to keep their options open.

Who can doubt that the permanent establishment of multiple freedoms has been the overriding consideration of political movements of different ideological hues in modern times? A massive amount of money is spent on campaigns to free groups of people from the scourges of insanitary housing, rampant diseases, illiteracy, polluted water supplies, ignorance about family planning, poor agricultural techniques, inadequate or unhealthy diets, lack of educational opportunities (especially for girls) and servile living conditions for wives.

Everywhere, freedom is coveted. Is it too much to postulate that, for modern human life, freedom (along with equality, with which it is closely linked) constitutes, maybe even defines, the most fundamental good? For, without freedom, it is not possible to pursue other worthwhile values in life. It is a value to be highly esteemed, experienced, endorsed and extended.

However, despite its high standing, how often do we, citizens of the modern world, pause to ask what precisely we mean by freedom? Is its meaning entirely self-evident? As in the cases of tolerance and equality, is there not more than a whiff of rhetoric in our many references to the term? On closer inspection, we find that people do not always mean the same thing; there are unresolved clashes of interpretation. What should count as freedom? Do we think, for example, of freedom wholly in terms of being liberated from external restraints? What place, if any, does the notion of an inner freedom play, where a person may be able to conquer various controlling habits, such as excessive drinking, smoking, compulsive eating, an unmanageable temper, jealousy and irrational fears? How does one link freedom to the great issues of life, such as personal identity, a sense of worth, the search for meaning, the inevitability of death, the nurture of children, cultural, religious and ethnic diversity? Rightly or wrongly, the pursuit, conquest and preservation of individual freedoms in a 'free' society seems to have become humanity's chief goal.

As an all-encompassing ideal, it has become an end worth pursuing for its own sake; not merely as a means to some other end.

This study of the uses and abuses of the concept of freedom will be based, to a considerable extent, on a book I wrote on the meaning of freedom, nearly two decades ago, which is now out of print.[18] It will be supplemented by attending to subsequent discussions provoked by changing public and private perceptions of freedom, not least in the area of freedoms of thought, conscience, religion, opinion, assembly and association, as laid out in Articles 18, 19 and 20 of the *Universal Declaration of Human Rights*. Despite the hyperbole that sometimes surrounds the notion of freedom, some see these freedoms as being under considerable threat, or even being eroded. They are being challenged by other values, such as those of non-discrimination, equality and rights, or by more recent perceptions of freedom, such as those coming from public intrusion into private lives, linguistic abuse, hurt feelings or insults. In recent times, these have been highlighted by an acrimonious debate around the protection and limitations of the freedom of the press.

Freedom is, undoubtedly, one of the major issues of our day. It is part of life, both in its presence and absence. In either preserving it or denying it, there are huge interests at stake. It is not surprising, therefore, that much controversy surrounds its implementation in public policies. Freedom, as we shall see, presents itself as a rather ambiguous reality, with many positive features, but also some destructive ones. The pursuit of freedom, in so far as it becomes a self-referring goal, can be self-defeating. It can only come into proper focus when set in the context of a higher good, which gives an adequate perspective for answering the question: freedom from and for what?

---

[18] Kirk, J. Andrew, *The Meaning of Freedom: A Study of Secular, Muslim and Christian Views*, (1998), Carlisle, Paternoster Press

The language of freedom

The burden of this book is that language influences culture and, in turn, is influenced by it. The extensive vocabulary associated with modern notions of freedom helps to extend and cement certain freedoms, whilst possibly devaluing others. A *pluralism*, or more correctly, plurality, of beliefs and *lifestyles* is something that most people have come to expect and accept. We acknowledge that *alternative* ways of looking at and relating to the world enrich life and our own appreciation of it.

Each person is said to live a *unique, autonomous* existence. They have a right to be free from the interference of others, as long as they respect other people's equal freedoms to the same extent. A free society is, almost by definition, a *permissive* one. What I do in my private life is my affair. Freedom should mean that I am allowed to occupy a certain space and time, *liberated* from invasion by the outside world, to live out my system of *values,* as I alone deem fit. It follows from this that a free society is one in which people are consciously *open-minded* about differences and *tolerant* of other people's choices.

In order to achieve an *egalitarian* society, one of the most important types of freedom is that of *free access to information.* This is not merely a passive freedom, in the sense that information should be in the public domain and easily available, but an active right in which, through educational systems and government initiatives, information becomes common property. Information is the gateway to intelligent *decision-making* and expanded *choice.*

Many social historians would say that the concept which most sharply sums up the modern passion for freedom is that of *individualism* (an emphasis on the priority of the individual's concerns over those of any community). *Self-determination* in the political sphere is unfinished business unless the individual is *emancipated* from the social pressures of group loyalty, with its often-subtle system of reward and punishment. This kind of communitarian pressure may be exercised to exert *control* over an individual's choice of what religion to follow, if any, whom to vote for, whom to marry, where to live and what kind of career to pursue. To be free is to be genuinely *independent*. In the last resort, freedom means accepting restrictions only on a purely *voluntary* basis.

A further complicating area of concern alongside the language of freedom is the freedom of language. Some maintain that communication is only possible in so far as a linguistic community preserves the traditional meaning of words and rules of grammar and recognises some supreme authority mandated with the task of adjudicating disputes. Others believe that strict adherence to inherited patterns of signification stultify *creative* thinking, *imaginative* story-telling and *expanding* vocabularies. Indeed, they might go as far as to say that attempting to define the parameters of freedom, in the case of language, in order to bring some kind of order to the diversity of understandings, is entirely misconceived and a lost cause; everyone should be at *liberty* to choose their own linguistic *options*.

Instances of freedom

Whatever may be the power of language and the expectations that it evokes, actual practice is more important. To a greater or lesser extent, tangible freedoms have increased in many societies during the last few decades. However, the expansion is disproportionate across the world; some have experienced much greater restrictions. Through the advent of modern medicine, many nations are relatively free from former killer diseases such as diphtheria, meningitis, scarlet fever, poliomyelitis, smallpox and tuberculosis.

In nations where per capita wealth has increased substantially, people are freer to travel. The tourist industry is one aspect of a leisure revolution. Leisure is freedom from what are, strictly speaking, tasks carried out that are necessary for existence. It is the sphere of relaxation, in which persons can choose to enjoy themselves in their own way. Come Friday evening, ideally, people are free (for two days), from everyday working life, to indulge their interests and hobbies. By referring to this space as 'the weekend', we demonstrate an interesting attitude to the relation between work and play; for the first five days of the week we earn 'a living', then comes the 'end of the week' when we are free to 'live' by what we have earned. The freedom of Friday to Sunday is made sweeter by the knowledge that we have already paid for the rest.

Wealth has also enabled sophisticated levels of technological innovation; it has transformed the realm of necessity into one of liberty. It offers freedom from financial anxiety through private and state provision against unforeseen and unwelcome events such as a protracted illness, the loss of employment, a divorce or forced early retirement. The possession and enjoyment of private property also helps to expand choice and increase security. This is an ideal picture. In reality, even in relatively affluent societies, the distribution of wealth is exceptionally uneven. Ambitious schemes to end poverty do not seem to achieve their goals. Freedom, in the sense of expanded opportunities for people to choose what they would like to do with their surplus earnings, is a long way from being enjoyed by whole populations. Nevertheless, it remains an aspiration, for the desire to be delivered from dependency on others is normally powerful.

Modern societies have helped to free individuals from the arbitrary and oppressive obligations formerly demanded by the communities into which they were born. So, freedom means liberation from the accident of birth, as a result of which people have been bound to observe the traditions, customs and regulations of past societies. The freedom to be different not only holds between cultures, but between generations from the same culture.

This new reality has been particularly liberating for women, traditionally confined to well-defined roles in the home on behalf of the family. The right to equal education, the pursuit of a career, the choice of whether, whom and when to marry, access to methods of family planning, paid maternity leave and free or cheap nursery provision for pre-school children has changed the lives and expectations of women.

Academic or intellectual freedom is highly prized, particularly in tertiary education. Freedom means that both staff and students are released from having to subscribe to either a set of religious beliefs or particular ideology before they can teach and study. The individual, at least in theory, is free to pursue his or her own line of investigation, even when that seems to go against currently received views in any particular discipline.

Gradually, over a period of some 400 years, freedom of conscience for the individual has become more respected. This respect has been built on the struggle for the free exercise of religion, on giving critical human reasoning priority over inherited dogmas, on the refusal to delegate moral responsibility to others and on the legally protected rights of minorities to dissent.

Modern people are not prepared to consent to an uncritical approval of tradition, customs or values, however venerable they may be. Every institution must be open to public scrutiny and debate. Any form of secrecy, special pleading of interest groups or the hint of cover-ups is especially suspect in the public's mind. Essentially, institutions (national and local governments, banks, medical and educational establishments, businesses and industries) and those that operate them are there to serve the needs of free people, and not the other way around. Freedom is ensured by making certain that the distinction is carefully maintained.

The advent of the World Wide Web and increasingly advanced technology has brought the freedom to know and communicate on a global stage. Even where essential freedoms, as we have been describing them, are severely restricted, it is hard for repressive regimes to block access to information available on countless websites, or through foreign or social media, text messages and electronic mail. It appears that even in relatively poor nations, many people possess computers and smart phones that are the gateways to information about everything one could possibly want to know. Freedom from ignorance or propaganda, especially when deliberately induced, is one of the main features of the contemporary world. It is one of the principle ways in which victims of injustice and oppression can be liberated from their circumstances.

A variety of perspectives

Over the course of many years, the concept of freedom has acquired a wide range of interpretations and applications, in both common and more reflective language. The idea of freedom, though treated with deep veneration, is much disputed.

A negative view

Many argue that freedom must be limited to its negative application; that is, freedom from any agent external to myself determining what is in my best interests and forcing me to comply. People are free to the extent that no individual or group interferes with their activities. To be prevented from doing what one would otherwise do, or to be restricted or hindered in doing it, is to be unfree, coerced or enslaved:

> "The only freedom which deserves the name is that of pursuing our own good in our own way."[19]

This view places emphasis on curbing all authority external to the individual. Freedom is genuine, when people's actions are truly their own, when they have not been persuaded

---

[19] Berlin I., (1969), *Four Essays on Liberty*, p. 127, Oxford, OUP.

against their wishes to believe or act in certain ways. The term often used for this belief about freedom is self-determination. It is the self alone that decides which boundaries to set to its actions. In the last analysis, a person is free only when able to will an action without pressure or duress.

This view of freedom is sometimes expressed in common jargon as the right to do as I please with my life, as long as I do not harm others. The unrestricted pursuit of individual happiness is legitimate, provided that the equally legitimate pursuits of others are not thereby infringed. This means that no one else can decide for me what constitutes my happiness, nor has the state any valid reason to arbitrate in my affairs. The state should not decide acceptable and unacceptable lifestyles, when these concern the mutually agreed decisions of responsible adults.

Three major assumptions underlie the negative concept of freedom. First, the scope of the state's legislative power over the individual should be restricted to a minimum. The state, as a collective entity, does not necessarily have a greater sense of what is morally right or wrong. Secondly, the sovereignty of the individual conscience must be allowed to reign supreme. One cannot be an authentic person unless one is at liberty to obey the dictates of one's own sense of right and wrong. Thirdly, because modern societies are pluralistic, options for the way one leads one's life should be equally valid, as far as the state is concerned.

A positive view

Many argue that freedom should mean much more than the absence of restraint. Non-coercion is only half the story; the other half concerns the expansion of choice. Freedom is really about possibilities and potency. The problem with the negative view is that it is reductionist, and therefore does not provide an adequate statement. Moreover, it is based on a dubious double negative – not being prohibited from a particular action.

Non-prohibition is quite different from acquiring a positive opportunity. For example, a person may be entirely free, in principle, to join a particular club (there are no limitations based on gender, race or age), but as the entrance fee and annual subscription are out of reach of most people, they are not, in reality, free to become members.

If freedom is the power to act according to what the will determines, then creating conditions that make a choice possible is part of actual freedom. (We have explored this concept in the context of equal opportunities). This is known as 'effective freedom.' If I need certain resources, powers or abilities in order to achieve self-realisation, then having these resources constitutes part of freedom itself. I am free to follow a particular profession, only if I have acquired the necessary qualifications, not because, in principle, there are no restrictions on who may enter. I am free to act as I want only if I have a proper chance to develop my capacities. Otherwise, freedom becomes a frustrating fiction.

Freedom also, in many cases, depends not only on a lack of constraints, but on the positive actions of others: freedom from sickness depends on the action of health professionals; freedom from the consequences of a lack of exercise depends, in part, on the availability of sports facilities publicly provided; freedom to breathe clean air depends on the enforcement of regulations restricting the toxic nature of exhaust fumes and the discharge of industrial gases.

Arguments in favour of positive freedoms are controversial, since they may require the curbing of some people's negative freedoms in the interests of a greater distribution of freedom for all – such as land reform to give more people a means of livelihood through agriculture, or the prohibition of smoking in confined spaces to free non-smokers from having to inhale other people's cigarette fumes. The supreme example, perhaps, is a government's responsibility to levy a tax on income or savings, in order that wealth may be better redistributed for the benefit of the majority.

To limit freedom to the negative idea is to be naïve about the place occupied by unequal power in determining choice. Most people judge instinctively that the non-restriction of freedoms (the negative view) can be achieved, ultimately, only by the extending of freedoms to as many as possible (the positive view). Otherwise, the meaning of freedom is ideologically determined by those who have the power to defend their own interests.

Other aspects of freedom

Modern notions of freedom are associated, not only with individual desires, political and economic ideas and movements, but with philosophical thought, artistic endeavour and spiritual experience.

Existential philosophy

One of the most potent expressions of human defiance against the creeping loss of freedom through intellectual conventions and bureaucratic controls has been existentialism. It has emerged as a serious statement about the reality of life in a universe that appears to be absurd. It has much in common with 'post-modern' thought.

Existentialism has made a particular view of freedom into one of its distinctive features. It both captures and promotes a distinct mood in the modern world. The modern person, it is asserted, experiences life as a series of unrelated encounters with the material world, unified neither by an integrated inner person, nor by an unchanging transcendent reality. On a naturalistic reading of humans' biological past, people are the result of chance; not an overriding, personal, conscious design built into their nature. This means that human beings do not possess a specific, given essence which precedes their actual, concrete action in the world.

Without an external reference point or even a stable, internal reference point, life is a ceaseless flux in which, potentially, meaning, purpose, moral values and human relations may change arbitrarily from day to day. No wonder, then, that whether a person considers themselves modern, post-modern or post-post-modern, many are going through a severe crisis of identity. This situation would seem to spell a complete loss of freedom, for freedom is related to what is *worth* choosing, but without an overall, given purpose in life, we cannot know what is worthwhile. It appears that every choice and action is equally meaningful and equally absurd.

The message of existentialism is that, precisely in this condition, the human being is radically free. The French philosopher, Jean-Paul Sartre, believed that, because we are devoid of a given constitution, over which we have no control, and because there is no god to provide us with values and commands, "we are left alone . . . That is what I mean when I say that man is condemned to be free."[20]

Freedom, then, is the decision to shoulder the full responsibility, despite the 'anguish', 'abandonment' and 'despair' implied in the human condition, of creating one's own meaning, values and being, by a voluntary act of the will. This action reminds one of the philosopher Kant's injunction, in defining 'enlightenment,' by "dare to know". The individual is alone and cannot blame anyone or anything else for what she or he is. Those who shelter behind the hand that fate has dealt them in life, fearful of the challenge of being absolutely free, Sartre accuses of having 'bad faith.' He reserves his scorn especially for those who submit to the imposed meanings and values of a culture captured and controlled by the media in all its forms.

Aesthetic freedom

All forms of art, if they are to be authentic, must originate in the spontaneous, imaginative side of human nature. Artists are

---

[20] *Existentialism as a Humanism*, (1956), quoted in Kauffmann, Walter (ed.), *Existentialism from Dostoevsky to Sartre,* pp. 287-311, New York, Meridian Books.

at liberty to use any style which suits their mood. Images may flow freely. Artists should impose their forms on the artistic medium being used, not because of some external compulsion to do so, but as an expression of individual choice. The viewer, or listener, also has the freedom to interpret the art-object as they deem fit.

In many ways, modern aesthetics is the child of successive romantic movements that have protested against an excessively rationalist notion of an objective, minutely ordered, intellectually accessible universe. Like the scientist, the artist may engage in constant experiment. Unlike the work of the scientist, however, there are no generally accepted criteria for validating results. There is thus a sense in which judgement, particularly moral, is out of place. We appreciate the artist's work according to individual taste and personal preference.

Art flows from the artist's experience of life, attempting to capture, in visual or audio means of communication, thought and emotions peculiar to the creative imagination of the person concerned. The only form of 'bad' art is that which is insincere and simply copies past styles or expresses other people's views. Art is corrupted when it is forced to express a certain ideology or conform to public opinion, or even the consensus of fellow artists.

The prevalent contemporary emphasis on the priority of personal experience as the starting place for making sense of reality, and the invitation to be in touch with one's feelings and impressions, are part of the heritage derived from romanticism. It fits well a culture convinced of the equal validity of all choices, all ways of expressing oneself, all patterns of believing and all ways of living; the hallmark of which is known as 'post-modernity'.

'Spiritual' freedom

Another way of coping with a world that seems to be unduly controlled by the rational management of time, talents and resources, does not seem to offer any alternative to ever-expanding economic growth and consumerism as the object of economic life, appears to be endemically brutal, incapable of resolving its mounting environmental crisis, and has given up on the search for a coherent and satisfying purpose for existence, is to retreat inwards.

The Stoics taught that we all possess an inner citadel, where we can be free from the pressures and seeming irrationalities of the most rational of predetermined existences. However circumscribed our life may be by the outward circumstances in which we live, and over which we have little control, within this inner sphere, we can dedicate ourselves to our own emancipation. Through activities such as meditation, right thinking, healthy eating, care for the environment, or perhaps belonging to small, intentional communities based on a particular form of 'spirituality,' individuals can transcend the limitations of a culture which appears to give precedence to the supreme value of material progress. They are, then, free, in so far as they have consciously chosen to reject a life dedicated to self-gratification.

In this view, freedom is not a commodity that someone else can give or withhold; it is something I lay hold of within myself. This kind of freedom can withstand situations where people are outwardly restrained. Thus, for example, when unjustly confined as a prisoner of conscience or when living in a 'surveillance' society, it is possible to be free, both from acquiescence in a political system that tramples on elementary freedoms, and from personal hatred and bitterness that engenders a destructive passion for revenge.

Some define 'spiritual' freedom in terms of the interaction between a supposed higher and lower nature. People cannot experience genuine freedom until they have come to terms with themselves. If they are not at ease with themselves, are unable to forgive themselves their failures, despise their inability to make genuine friendships, are frustrated by the weakness of their will, irrational fantasies and inhibitions and are fearful of breaking free from conventional norms, they are not in control of themselves. The truly free person is one who is confident about their goals in life and able to fulfil them. Such a person would be in control of his or her own intellectual processes of reflection, memory of the past and imagination of the future. A person cannot claim to be free unless they can reflect on their lower impulses, criticise them rationally and do something about transforming them. Freedom is experienced in the act of knowing and coming to terms with oneself, and then changing oneself to the person one really longs to be.

Obstacles to freedom

Protest against authority

Despite the constraints of a largely impersonal economic system, sinister tendencies towards limiting civil liberties and recent attempts to demonstrate that human decisions are merely the result of complex biological programming, human freedom is a reality. Nevertheless, it is not a commodity that is available without limitation. It could be that real freedom is found in understanding and accepting the proper limits to freedom.

Freedom, in the modern sense, is largely a result of the rejection of an externally imposed authority: whether that of an autocratic state, ruled by a king or emperor with presumed divine rights, an undivided church or the teaching of the Bible. The result was the decline of a 'public, transcendent God' and the rise of numerous 'private, immanent gods', fashioned according to the perceived needs of a new kind of world in the making.

The idea of the good became disconnected from the hypothesis of a personal God and was seen to be resting on a foundation either of natural rights or utility. Evil was believed to be located in the deep recesses of the human spirit and identified with imperfections in human development, often due to abusive relationships suffered in childhood. Frequently, the perpetrators of violence are those who have been victims of it.

Under pressure from the modern scientific world-view, theism became deism; resulting from an enclosed rationalism, deism became agnosticism or atheism. The philosophers of the Enlightenment, to their own satisfaction, rendered God innocuous. But, like Macbeth, they did not realise that the universe would rebel at the deed. Nietzsche, some one hundred years later, replaced self-satisfied atheism with agonised atheism, and, in his own self, suffered the consequences. As a result of the 'decline of God,' some see clear symptoms of the 'decline of the West.'

Freedom from God has led to a desire to be free from an innate human nature. A natural, inborn human essence, necessary to make sense of human rights, has been considered too restrictive of the free flow of the human spirit. Creativity, spontaneity and authenticity depend on a notion of human nature repeatedly 'in the making.'

Out of this determination was born the voluntarist tradition of human moral discourse. The transcendent is a delusion. Yet, because reason, observing the natural order, cannot transcend itself, it has been unable to explain how human beings, alone of all living creatures, can, nevertheless, contemplate themselves. Bound by a purely materialist view of existence, humans have incarcerated themselves in a room without doors or windows.

Substitution of belief in divine revelation by the doctrine of a closed natural order is proving to be a high price to pay for the freedom to remain autonomous. Contrary to some contemporary intellectual fashions, the latter is probably less empirically based than the former. Rebellion against what can be denied (an innate nature common to all humans) but not fundamentally changed is a futile exercise in self-emancipation. The true freedom is to recognise and live on the basis of a freedom limited by our ('given') nature and by the consequences of corruption committed by humans.

The disintegration of the self

One of the greatest challenges to real freedom is the failure to find a satisfying unity of being which does justice to the whole experience of life. What is needed is an over-arching theory which cannot only account for the successes of scientific enterprises, but also explain human moral sensitivity, discover a purpose that gives meaning to human achievements, satisfy a longing for community and enduring relationships and account for reflective intelligence and the sense of awe and thanksgiving evoked by the sheer wonder of the universe. The integration of the self depends, in large measure, on knowing *who we are* and *what we are for*.[21]

When exclusion from the meaning of things becomes too hard to bear, when autonomy leads to anomie, when self-created goals become mutually self-defeating and end up in self-recrimination, when the emotions and will can no longer cope with a world the intellect has failed to understand, some turn to various forms of mystical experience in an attempt to discover a coherence and significance for their lives and that of the wider world. However, mysticisms dissolve the unity in diversity of the relationship God-humanity-cosmos. The result is a conflation of two of the three elements – either God and humanity, humanity and the cosmos or God and the cosmos – in various forms of pantheism. The price paid for the failure to embrace a world-view that offers an authentic unifying principle is the loss of the person and the disintegration of the distinction between reality and illusion.

Freedom may mean, for some, that they can now enact their own story, unencumbered by outdated religions, philosophies and ideologies. However, there is no knowing

---

[21] In a forthcoming book, I have explored, in a series of historical cameos, the reality of what it means to be human. See, Kirk, J. Andrew, (2019), *Being Human: An Historical Inquiry into Who We Are*, Eugene OR: Wipf and Stock.

whether any of these personal stories may be significant, for they have become detached from history, culture and community. If community, beliefs and situations, hitherto deemed to have permanent validity, are considered a restriction on the liberty to create endlessly new worlds, there is no ultimate way of being able to distinguish what appears to the individual to be the case and what is actually the case. Having no fixed and continuous centre to one's life is a high price to pay for this version of freedom.

The relativity of perspectives

In educating the young into the requirements of good citizenship, there is much confusion, in modern societies, about the nature of moral values and how they should be taught. The inevitable consequence of freedom as autonomy is the reluctance to emphasise any particular foundation for morals or the inability to give an adequate reason for preferring one set of values to others. The great enemy of freedom to make up one's own mind, even from a young age, is assumed to be indoctrination – the inculcation of particular beliefs and values in a way which undermines pupils' capacity to reflect critically on these matters and come to their own genuine conclusions.

Such a view seems to be incontestable. To attempt to force personal preferences upon pupils is to treat them without proper respect; as means and not ends in themselves. However, there is both a methodological problem and a hidden agenda in this line of reasoning. The problem lies in the undoubted fact that people have no means of thinking for themselves or making up their own minds on the basis of raw information or the multiplicity of conflicting opinions. In real life, indirect indoctrination, through the views of parents and families, the pressure of peer groups, the reading of text books, the opinions of broadcasters and commentators, and the views and attitudes of respected cult heroes is going on the whole time.

Paradoxically, there are certain matters about which a pupil, apparently, is not allowed, by the educational system, to form his or her own opinion: for example, to come to the conclusion, after critical thought based on a coherent moral outlook, that the only proper context for intimate sexual activity is a permanent, monogamous, heterosexual relationship. In a relativistic age, such a position is considered far too dogmatic. So, sex education has to emphasise that pupils are at liberty to choose a number of options, according to what they feel comfortable with, whilst warning them of the damage they may incur by casual and 'unsafe' sex. Apart from this, all pupils have a duty to be tolerant of other's lifestyles. Logically, this approach to education simply conceals an alternative dogma, based on an alternative set of absolutes, and therefore, by any other name, is also indoctrination.

The hidden agenda behind the commitment to a policy of apparent open-mindedness is concealed in what is not said. A disguised form of indoctrination can happen through omission, when some arguments are excluded or are misrepresented, because they do not fit what the teacher, or the educational establishment, considers appropriate. Thus, education for good citizenship can take the form of drilling pupils into the belief that there is no alternative to an economic system based on perpetual growth, generated by competitive international free trade, and that learning is principally designed to enable them to participate successfully in the highly combative world of the job market. Education into 'free choice' appears to be education into the supreme values of global capitalism.

Freedom and state coercion

We come back to the beginning. On the one hand, we have an ideal of freedom as deliverance from the interference of politicians, as legislators, in the decisions that autonomous individuals are able to make on their own authority and in their own interests. On the other hand, freedom to form one's own opinions and act on them, in societies that lack any common ground for distinguishing right and wrong, leads, inevitably, to a conflict of ideas and pursuits that clash and have to be resolved by the community at large.

The powerful inclination of modern societies to ascribe only a relative value to all beliefs and actions makes their coherent functioning extremely difficult. This is the fundamental dilemma of cultures that believe freedom is only possible where all claims to ultimate and definitive truth are rejected. Nevertheless, reasons for scepticism about truth claims are understandable. There is the fear that truth claims are excuses for imposing arbitrary norms on society. There is the belief that they represent an implicit (spiritual or emotional) violence, because they imply that other people's contrary ideas do not have integrity or value. They seem to presume a superior understanding or knowledge about life, leading, possibly, to judgemental and condemnatory attitudes to others that will violate their self-esteem. They appear to preclude a sensitive listening to other views, especially from those with different histories and cultures. Therefore, they hinder the expansion of horizons and the learning of new insights. They tend to reflect closed minds, insulating people from the dread of doubt and uncertainty in a confusing world.

These considerations have become part of the warp and woof of modern societies. They are widely accepted as a correct assessment of the possibilities and limitations inherent in knowing. And yet, contrary to what might be expected, a relativism of beliefs does not enhance, but is inimical, to genuine freedom. The reason for this is quite simple. A society cannot allow a clash of moral beliefs and practices, if there are no adequate grounds for determining what is permissible and what is forbidden. To avoid a chaotic free-for-all, boundaries have to be set. Now, boundaries depend on there being moral absolutes, so that certain actions are presumed to be wrong, whatever the circumstances – murder, deceit, theft, cruelty, false testimony, slavery, brutal aggression, to name a few. However, if no beliefs can justify their claim to be true, modern, secular and pluralist societies have a dilemma: where can they find a reliable source for these absolutes?

A choice has to be made. In the past, moral teaching has been largely based on religious beliefs. The mere existence of the latter does not, of course, guarantee the validity and cogency of the morality that has emanated from them. Religions, unfortunately, have sanctioned horrendous practices, and continue, in some instances, to do so. It is tempting, therefore, to ditch all religious input into debates about morality and start again. This is what secular societies and humanist associations would advocate: freedom of religion is interpreted as freedom from religion, at least in the public square. However, if truth is not available in the field of moral values, because all beliefs are relative to time and place, whence comes the notion that freedom is an essential good, which must be protected?

In the absence of a convincing ground for moral absolutes, the state is bound to act arbitrarily, making up moral values as it goes along. Freedoms, then, become subject to the will of the legislating powers and judiciary systems of a nation or, in the case of the European Union, a group of nations. This is exactly what seems to be happening. Without any fundamental moral foundations, freedoms are being sorted into categories and given unequal status.

The result is that certain freedoms are under attack and being diminished. The highest profile cases are probably freedom of expression and freedom to act in accordance with one's core beliefs. It is now possible to compile a list of beliefs and actions that are, according to an implicit moral consensus of a particular opinion-forming group of influential thinkers, deemed either acceptable or inadmissible, as the case may be. Interestingly enough, most of these have to do with the current abuse of the language of tolerance, equality, freedom and rights, as exposed in this study.

Freedom of expression

Allowing every citizen of a democratic society the freedom to express their most cherished beliefs, and to act in accordance with them, throws up a whole host of controversial issues. It is one thing, for example, to declare magnanimously that everyone is free to believe what they like – in a flat earth, in extra-terrestrial visitors to this planet, that the holocaust under the Nazis never happened, that it is possible to communicate with the dead, that it is justifiable to abort babies on grounds of being the 'wrong' sex, and other fanciful notions – it is another to allow them to disseminate such beliefs, or even more contentiously, to permit them to act on the basis of them.

However, freedom to believe, if it does not entail freedom to express that belief publicly and to act consistently with it, is a pig's ear. Nevertheless, although some eccentric or preposterous beliefs may be quite harmless, for they do not lead to any damaging or dangerous consequences for society as a whole, there are others that, if practised, would cause much distress and suffering. It is one thing, for example, for small minorities of people in modern societies to believe in the supremacy of some races over others. It is another that they be allowed to form political parties, or even civil societies, to campaign for this view, and, in the unlikely event of being elected into office, carry out policies that exclude certain races from full participation in society. Towards apartheid policies of any ideological hue, the only possible moral and political response is intolerance and prohibition.

Some adherents of one religion in particular believe that the god they worship requires all human communities to be governed by a set of laws that its religious leaders, over centuries, have codified through systems of jurisprudence. The laws are intended to provide a common framework that governs personal, family and social practices for all. In multicultural, pluralist societies, the religious believers in question may aspire to the implementation of their ideal; they may even promote such a model of society as being the best possible. However, it is hard to see how 'secular' societies could ever allow them to be in a position to carry out their beliefs, even were it to be in a limited way, within their own community of faith.

These two examples counter the common assumption that the state, for fear of discriminating against a particular concept of equal rights and treatment, has to accord equal validity to all beliefs. Undoubtedly, at times, it stands between 'the devil and the deep blue sea.' On the one hand, a society's acceptance of a plurality of beliefs means that the burden of proof on restrictions of freedom of expression and action lies with those who pass laws and those who administer them. Freedoms of conscience and conscientious objection are precious prerogatives, for which many in the past have sacrificed much to achieve; they must be carefully monitored and protected at all times. On the other hand, championing freedoms does not imply that anything is allowable. The law already recognises this, in the cases of libel and defamation of character against individuals and incitement to hatred and violence against specific groups of people. Interestingly, it is much more equivocal when it comes to defamation against group beliefs, such as religions. Thus, for example, the public's contemptuous mocking of key religious figures such as Jesus or Muhammad is not prohibited, even though its motivation may be to promote hate and hostility towards Christians and Muslims.

Freedom of religion

Some recent, highly controversial court cases have highlighted enormous sensitivities in the realm of freedom of conscience in the context of religious convictions. Two areas of deep concern have come to the fore in recent years: freedom of conscience and equality laws and freedom to display religious symbols and wear certain kinds of religiously-associated clothing.

These are much disputed questions. Space does not allow anything like a full treatment; only a few points can be mentioned briefly. Firstly, beliefs cannot be divorced from their practice. Beliefs that do not demand action are defective and unsatisfactory; not to act on them signals their unimportance. Freedom to act on one's beliefs is the only freedom worth having.

Secondly, however, not all manifestations of religion are acceptable. Fatwas that sanction the killing of the opponents of a religion cannot be tolerated, for the prohibition on murder is absolute. This may be an extreme case.

Nevertheless, thirdly, those manifestations of religion allowable in public will be a contentious issue in a secular society. Recently, a number of street preachers have been arrested, just because a passer-by reported them to the police for proclaiming a message they personally found offensive. Only a few have subsequently been charged with any offence; without exception, they have been told there is no charge to answer. Society must decide exactly what people have the freedom to declare in public.

In this context, fourthly, society has a duty to distinguish, if necessary, between an individual's stated beliefs and those of respected authorities who speak on behalf of the faith in question. One cannot claim, on behalf of a religion, a purely personal interpretation:

> "If...a religious practice is created only by individual belief, rather than by communal understandings, anything can become religious, and the idea of religion as deserving special protection becomes meaningless."[22]

Even worse is to burden the legal system with the task of deciding which aspects of a religion's beliefs are a core part

---

[22] Trigg, Roger, (2012), *Equality, Freedom and Religion*, Oxford, OUP, p. 105.

of the faith. Judges are not trained in theological disciplines and are, therefore, ill-equipped to give rulings in controversial cases.

Fifthly, those cases, where freedom of religion appears to clash with other freedoms, are particularly contentious. These have been highlighted by recent equalities legislation, where refusal to carry out public duties on behalf of statutory bodies for reasons of religious conscience has been deemed unacceptably discriminatory. One case in point was the refusal of a registrar for marriages to conduct ceremonies for two people of the same sex. Her objection met the criterion of communal belief; most religions have stated that same-sex civil partnerships or marriages contravene their fundamental beliefs. It is true that she was practising discrimination. However, as we have seen, discrimination can be a positive virtue, when it is interpreted as discernment. It happens in all walks of life; particularly in choosing between people for a certain job. In the case of the registrar, it could be argued that she be accorded the freedom to discriminate in a matter where she and her co-religionists believe that same-sex unions, however legal, damage public morality.

Some will say that she had the right to refuse to conduct marriage ceremonies in certain cases, but that, nevertheless, the authorities were bound to uphold the law by insisting that she carried out her contracted duties. Her options, if she wished to follow her conscience, were to disregard the law and take the consequences (almost certainly dismissal from her job) or resign. Others will say that a negative attitude to homosexual relations is so central to religious belief that her convictions in this instance should be accommodated. Where conscience clashes with a rigid interpretation of equality rights, a certain amount of latitude should be practised. Freedom of religion should not be equated with freedom to be unemployed.

Another case concerns a private, commercial confectionery business which refused to take an order for a cake, when the stipulation was that the wording on the top should promote homosexual relations. Again, refusal to comply with the request was interpreted as unacceptable discrimination on the grounds of the couple's sexual orientation and was reported to the Equality Commission. This is quite a different case from the preceding one. Public institutions are not directly involved; no employment law is being contravened. More importantly, a commercial enterprise surely has the freedom to decide what it is going to produce and for whom; otherwise, economic freedoms are being trampled on by imposing arbitrary business restrictions.

The firm concerned could have been less forthright and simply said that it could not make the cake, because it already had too many orders on its books. Moreover, as in the case of proprietors of a bed and breakfast business who, because of their Christian convictions, did not permit a same-sex couple to sleep together in their house, it would seem that the request for the cake was not genuine, but a deliberately provocative attempt to set a trap by challenging the limits of religious freedom. Discrimination is a blunt instrument to be used as an argument that trumps all else, for it works in more than one direction. If it is illegal, on the grounds of race, gender, age, sexuality or disability to discriminate against equality legislation, why is it legal, on grounds of religion, to discriminate?[23]

It is to the credit of the British government, in the context of what constitutes discrimination, that having steered a highly controversial Bill through Parliament to legalise same-sex marriage, it has made clear that teachers, paid by the state, are not obligated in class to uphold its moral legitimacy. This represents a good example of accommodation to the reasonable demands of conscience backed by fundamental convictions about what is ultimately true. In this case, freedom

---

[23] The case was finally settled by the high court in favour of the confectionery business, on the ground that the refusal to bake the cake was not aimed at rejecting the couple's sexuality but at denying the request to promote homosexual marriage.

for a well-reasoned defence of conscience, on the grounds of a religiously-supported (but not only religious) moral stance, has been accommodated; at least for the time being.[24]

In a pluralist society of different beliefs and practices, where there are no concerns about the physical integrity of individuals, harm to communities or security of the state, freedom of action on the basis of a well-argued defence of conscience should be the default position of the law. In other words, governments whose legislation effectively constrains freedom of conscience have a burden of proof to show that restricting freedom really promotes the common good. In the light of recent statements on the need to promote core social values in a democratic society, there may be a conflict of policies at this point; unless, of course, freedom of conscience is not considered such a core value!

In regard to the wearing of certain items of clothing or religious symbols, the same default position should apply in most cases. To ban the wearing of a cross by people in public employment, whilst allowing other religious symbols to be displayed through clothing or adornments, is manifestly discriminatory. What right does a judge have to say, for example, that wearing a cross is not essential to Christian belief? If it is offensive to some, then in this case, it just has to be offensive. The wearing of grotesque masks at Halloween (a symbol surviving from past pagan beliefs) is offensive to Christians, yet they do not lobby for them to be banned.

The one exception to the general rule of freedom and tolerance is the complete covering of the face by some Muslim women. Whether or not the hijab (burqa, chador or niqab) is primarily a symbol of a woman's unacceptable subordination to and oppression by a male-dominated society is open to debate. A woman should be allowed to use clothing to cover

---

[24] As general acceptance by the public of same-sex marriage has bedded in, upholding the freedom of conscience not to have to teach its moral legitimacy is beginning to weaken.

her whole body if, for her, it is a symbol of modesty, privacy and the rejection of the sexualisation of the female body; likewise, if it genuinely marks an assertion of Islamic identity. However, the covering of the face, so that the person behind the veil is unrecognisable, is a step too far in an open society. For reasons of optimum communication and security, the face, which identifies the person and expresses their individual personality, must be visible. To hide one's face is to cut oneself off from proper human interaction, to imprison oneself in an unreal world and to withdraw from society. In the last analysis, it dehumanises the person concerned. Therefore, calls for the complete covering of the face to be banned in public on grounds of transparency may well be justifiable.

Conclusion

This survey of the meanings of freedom has shown, I believe, that any definition or understanding of freedom that seeks to make it fit all cases can only lead to an abuse of the concept and the reality. Above all, the long struggle for individual and, perhaps to a lesser extent, communal freedoms, against the tendency of public power to want to keep them under strict surveillance and restrict their implementation, has a history. The famous remark of John Curran has proved to be true time and time again:

> "The condition upon which God hath given liberty to man is eternal vigilance; which condition if he break, servitude is at once the consequence of his crime, and the punishment of his guilt."[25]

Freedom is a more precious commodity than many people realise. Of course, in practice, it can be abused. Freedom is

---

[25] Speech on the Right of Election of Lord Mayor of Dublin, 10th July 1790.

not the equivalent of licence, anarchy or complete self-determination. In order to be considered one of the most supreme virtues, ultimately worth dying for, it must be exercised with responsibility and discernment. Centralising powers, which are by nature fearful of conceding freedoms to individuals and civil organisations, are always looking for excuses to curtail its reach. A constant debate in the public realm, therefore, about the proper use and abuse of the language of freedom will be part of the eternal vigilance that keeps servitude at bay.

Select bibliography

Anderson, N., (1988), *Freedom under the Law: The Role of Law in Man's Quest for Freedom*, Eastbourne, Kingsway

Berlin, Irving, (1969), *Four Essays on Liberty*, Oxford, OUP

Carter, Ian, Kramer, Matthew H. and Steiner, Hillel (eds.), (2007), *Freedom: A Philosophical Anthology*, Oxford, Blackwell

Freire, Paolo, (1972), *Cultural Action for Freedom*, Harmondsworth, Penguin Books

Fromm, Eric, (2001/2), *The Fear of Freedom*, London, Routledge

Honneth, Alex, (2014), *Freedom's Right: The Social Foundations of Democratic Life*, Cambridge, Polity Press

Kant, Immanuel, (1995),'What is Enlightenment?' in *The Portable Enlightenment*, Harmondsworth, UK, Penguin Books

Kirk, J. Andrew, (1998), *The Meaning of Freedom: A Study of Secular, Muslim and Christian Views*, Carlisle, Paternoster Press

Raz, Joseph, (1986), *The Morality of Freedom*, Oxford, OUP

Sen, Amartya, (1999), *Development as Freedom,* Oxford, OUP

Trigg, Roger, (2007), *Religion in Public Life: Must Faith be Privatised?* Oxford, OUP

Trigg, Roger, (2012), *Equality, Freedom and Religion,* Oxford, OUP

CHAPTER 5

Rights and Obligations

"Nothing in this Declaration may be interpreted as implying for any State, group or person any right to engage in any activity or to perform any act aimed at the destruction of any of the rights and freedoms set forth herein" (Article 30, the *Universal Declaration of Human Rights, UDHR*)

Preliminary remarks

Over thirty years ago, I wrote an article on human rights for a symposium.[26] Perhaps surprisingly, I still agree, in general, with the sentiments I expressed at that time. However, there is at least one major aspect of my past thinking that I now want to challenge. At that time, I took for granted that the whole notion of human rights was valid. So, I began the article with a reference to the tireless work of Amnesty International in defence of prisoners of conscience, whose human rights have been denied by "the suspension of Habeas Corpus, imprisonment without trial, house arrests, deportation, physical assault and systematic torture."[27] (I still support, with thankfulness, all organisations striving to counter the abuse of morally justifiable human freedoms by political authorities of whatever ideological hue).

---

[26] See Kirk, J. Andrew, (1983), 'Human Rights: The Personal Debate' in Stott, John (ed.), *The Year 2000 AD*, pp. 1-26, Basingstoke, Marshalls.
[27] 'Human Rights', p. 1.

In the article, I went on to describe some of the current abuses of human rights, trying to be even-handed between regimes in different parts of the world. Only much later in the discussion did I suggest that the very idea of human rights might itself be problematical. Nevertheless, I ended up much as I had begun, with the assumption that human rights are self-explanatory and self-vindicating. Some recent applications of human rights discourse, enacted in legislation by Western governments and the European Parliament, have made me think again.

I have been particularly struck by the way in which the notion has been extended to more and more instances, so that almost anything that an individual or interest group feels aggrieved at becomes a claim that their natural rights are being ignored or trampled on.

Likewise, almost anything individuals or groups desire strongly enough becomes a rights' entitlement. So, the slow creep of human rights' demands has become a major concern as more and more legislation is enacted to protect people from alleged acts of discrimination or the removal of the privileges they assert belong to them 'by right'. Allied to this expansion of claims and counter-claims is the observation that alleged human rights often conflict. Thus, in order to end one kind of discrimination, a law is passed that may well create another.

A third major misgiving concerns the very concept of human rights. Do rights actually exist? Where has the idea come from? On what basis can they be justified? In the discussion that follows, I will explore the important issues of the extent of rights and the clash of rights. However, they cannot be settled until, and unless, the question about the existence of rights in the first place is cleared up.

Jeremy Bentham, an 18th century English philosopher and jurist and the father of utilitarianism as a moral principle, once remarked that talk of natural rights is "nonsense upon stilts."[28]

---

[28] Bowring, J. (ed.), (1838-43), *The Works of Jeremy Bentham*, p. 501, Edinburgh, William Tait.

In a critical analysis of the French *Declaration of Rights*, formulated in 1791, he concludes that the Declaration confuses arguments in favour of the necessity of rights with evidence for their actual reality. Others have voiced similar opinions. For example, Alasdair MacIntyre, a British moral philosopher, refers to the notion of human rights as a fiction, on the same level as belief in witches or unicorns, since there are no good grounds, either in theory or practice, for demonstrating their existence.[29]

The meaning of human rights

In common parlance, human rights are understood to imply that human beings, in certain instances, possess justified claims that entitle them, either as individuals or as a well-defined group, to require certain behaviour from others. In an analysis of the language of rights, they are usually separated into four different kinds. Firstly, there are *claims* for certain entitlements made by one human agent, which generates a corresponding duty on the part of another to make good those claims. Thus, for example, the right of a woman to receive equal pay for doing the same job as a man is a claim upon the employers to honour the principle of gender equality. Secondly, certain *powers* are claimed as the right to be able to effect certain actions without hindrance from third parties. In the case of property, for example, the owner claims the right to dispose of it freely as he or she wishes. Thirdly, there are *liberties*, i.e. the right to be free from certain obligations of the law. A classical case would be that of conscientious objection to a general draft of young people into the armed forces. Fourthly, there are *immunities*, meaning the right of people individually or collectively to be protected in certain circumstances against general principles like non-discrimination. Thus, a school with

---

[29] See *After Virtue*, (1985), p. 69, London, Duckworth.

a religious foundation, in the event of appointing a head teacher, would have the right to ignore legislation that requires non-discrimination of an applicant for the post on the basis of religious views.

Rights are assumed to be inherent, somehow, in the nature of things. They exist prior to and independently of the power of a state over its citizens. Thus, they exert a counter-balancing authority over the particular whims of a political administration by demanding implicitly that the latter adheres to the precepts supposedly enshrined in their universal claims. Rights should inform and shape legislation, rather than being granted or conceded by executive state power. Whether or not a particular government recognises rights is irrelevant, since it does not have the capacity to grant or withhold certain entitlements. It is in the context of authoritarian states, which seek to suspend normal civil guarantees to life, justice and liberty, that human rights' campaigns have become most incisive.

The origin of the concept of rights

It is commonplace to observe that, prior to about 1400 in Western Europe, "no expression in any ancient or modern language. . .could be correctly translated by the modern term 'a right'":

> "The concept began to appear in philosophical, political and legal discourse from roughly the time of the Renaissance onwards. It is tied to notions of the autonomy and liberty of the individual in relation to an absolute divine moral law as this was mediated by either Catholic or Protestant hegemonic states."[30]

---

[30] Kirk, J. Andrew (2007), *The Future of Reason, Science and Faith: Following Modernity and Postmodernity*, p. 191, Aldershot, Ashgate Publishing.

The idea was debated in 16th century Spain, especially in the University of Salamanca and in the writings of Fray Bartolome de Las Casas, in regard to the treatment of indigenous peoples in the Americas after the Spanish conquest.[31] The concept took on a life of its own during the controversies of the 16th and 17th centuries, regarding freedom of religion and conscience:

"The language of rights entered the United States bloodstream precisely because Dissenters left Britain in the search for freedom to worship. . .From this pressure came a more general language of rights which found expression in the emancipatory discourse of the eighteenth century, and particularly in political radicals like Tom Paine."[32]

Significantly, however, as the concept of rights began to develop, it lost its original foundation in the notion that individual conscience must be free to refuse the arbitrary interpretation of civic duties by unrepresentative authorities of the state. Conscience had appealed to the higher authority of the will of God, as manifested in his written word. With the coming of the self-styled 'Age of Reason,' divine law was transmuted into natural law built upon an assumed innate constitution or essence inhering in human beings as such.

It is within this secular tradition that the Preamble to the *Universal Declaration* begins with the words, "whereas recognition of the inherent dignity and of the equal and inalienable rights of all members of the human family is the foundation of freedom, justice and peace in the world. . ." It has come to be taken for granted that rights are a given fact of nature that do not have to be authorised or sanctioned by some temporal power, but discovered in the very reality of

---

[31] See Ruston, Roger (2004), *Human Rights and the Image of God*, London, SCM Press.
[32] Gorringe, T. J. (2004), *Furthering Humanity: A Theology of Culture*, p. 230, Aldershot, Ashgate Publishing.

being human. Seeing that the intrinsic, inalienable and absolute nature of human rights has been contested by philosophers, jurists, theologians and others, and seeing that the notion itself begs the question as to its derivation, defenders of the concept have elaborated a number of reasons to justify it.

The basis for the concept of human rights

In order for an analysis of the concept of rights to be as rigorous as possible, it is necessary to treat its current defence in a secular environment within in its own terms. This means refraining, initially, from introducing theological categories into the argument. A contemporary secular person argues that belief in God is unnecessary for a consistent, serious, morally-upright life. In a self-confessedly polemical book, the philosopher Anthony Grayling says,

> "religion (he is referring to Christianity) is precisely the wrong resource for thinking about moral issues in the contemporary world, and indeed subverts moral debate."

He then goes on to state the fundamental assumption which guides his ethical outlook:

> "Human beings are natural entities, intelligent animals, part of the order of nature. . .Recognition of these facts has given rise to the view that the kinds of problem faced both by individuals and societies are for this reason best handled naturalistically, and by reference to the actual experience and needs of mankind."[33]

Apart from the fact that this statement is asserted rather than argued, he does not seem to understand that both

---

[33] *What is Good? The Search for the Best Way to Live*, (2003), p. 69, London, Weidenfeld and Nicolson.

experience and needs have to be interpreted from a perspective which should be justified, not simply stated. Clearly, he has accepted, as a premise, what he needs to demonstrate, namely that (a) the whole religious experience of the human race is either irrelevant or false, (b) one can make sense of life in all its complexity from a perspective that completely excludes any extra-mundane information, and (c) derive, from within an externally unguided human reason, ethical norms for a good life. Grayling spends most of his book ridiculing, through gross misrepresentation, the truth claims of the Christian message. He hardly begins to lay the foundations for an alternative, humanistic ethic.[34]

If he were to attempt such a task, he would have to start from his own premise that human beings are to be understood wholly from within a naturalistic framework. This means that everything that apparently makes humans distinct from every other living organism – consciousness, conscience, rationality, linguistic communication, the ability to plan for the future, the drive to ask questions about meaning and right and wrong behaviour, the appreciation of beauty, and indeed the intimation that, without a transcendent direction, life is absurd – is the result of an evolutionary process that has operated since the dawn of time, purely by chance, without any kind of supervision and having no purpose in view, except survival and the ability to reproduce. In the face of the alternative theistic account of human origins, the naturalistic view is simply asserted dogmatically. The contention between the two views can only be settled by considering which one gives

---

[34] Grayling continues to argue, along the same lines, for a consistently secular humanistic ethic in a subsequent book, *The God Argument: The Case Against Religion and for Humanism* (2013), London, Bloomsbury. In my forthcoming book, *Being Human: An Historical Inquiry Into Who We Are* (2019), Eugene, OR, Wipf and Stock, I contend that secular humanism as a world-view does not fulfill its claim to possess a coherent set of beliefs about moral action; see, chapter 10, "Human Existence in the Thought of Secular Humanism".

the best explanation of the total reality of human life, of being able to answer most convincingly the most fundamental questions that humans, in their more reflective moods, ask about their existence.

A secular, humanistic ethic has accepted severe constraints on its thinking. This affects its ability to make sense of human rights' discourse. Yet, in the modern world, this is where the discussion begins and ends. Religious perspectives are considered unwelcome. This is partly due to the fact that, in contemporary Western culture, politicians and legislators have been conditioned to shape and interpret policies in the belief that pluralism is the supreme social reality to consider:

> "...this principle...is pivotal to the very possibility of the existence of populous, multi-ethnic, multicultural societies of the kind now standard in the West."[35]

One of the main problems with this position is that a secular perspective, as a self-justifying claim to neutrality between different religious beliefs, is erected into the norm that has the right to adjudicate ethical values and practices. However, clearly it is not neutral. Defining itself against religious worldviews, it possesses its own philosophical justification and political agenda. Both of these are disputable on the basis of both faith and reason.

In the context of our discussion, it is interesting to note that Grayling's only reference to human rights in his entire book comes in the allusion to tolerance:

> "One way of enshrining tolerance in a firmer and more explicit set of principles has been the institution of national and international frameworks of human rights."[36]

---

[35] *What is Good?*, p. 69.
[36] *What is Good?*, p. 69.

However, for reasons that we will explore later, the enactment of human rights can, in some circumstances, increase intolerance.

The first systematisation of the notion of human rights is usually credited to the Dutch philosopher and jurist Hugo Grotius, who derived them from his defence of the concept of natural law:

"In the first few sections of the "Prolegomena," (to his work, *De iure belli ac pacis libri tres* (Paris: Buon, 1625)) Grotius lays the groundwork for his natural law theory. Then, in section eleven, he writes that 'What we have been saying would have a degree of validity even if we should concede. . .that which cannot be conceded without the utmost wickedness, that there is no God, or that the affairs of men are of no concern to him.' Instead of emerging from or being otherwise dependent on God, the fundamental principles of ethics, politics and law obtain in virtue of nature. As he says, 'the mother of right — that is, of natural law — is human nature' (Prol. §16). Somewhat later, he clarifies why it is that human nature produces the natural law: 'The law of nature is a dictate of right reason, which points out that an act, according as it is or is not in conformity with rational nature, has in it a quality of moral baseness or moral necessity; and that, in consequence, such an act is either forbidden or enjoined' (I.1.10.1). If an action agrees with the rational and social aspects of human nature, it is permissible; if it doesn't, it is impermissible (cf. I.1.12.1). That is to say, the source of the natural law is the (in)compatibility of actions with our essences as rational and social beings."[37]

In other words, rights are justified by virtue of human nature. They can be known by the light of human reason, independently of belief in God:

---

[37] Miller, Jon, 'Grotius' in *Stanford Encyclopedia of Philosophy* (www.stanford.edu/entries/grotius)

"The notion of universal, inviolable human rights – now enshrined in many international treaties, declarations and legal frameworks – owes much to the kind of natural rights theory that stems from Grotius."[38]

This presumption might be called, 'the *intuitive* theory': repeated cognitive insight in all ages and across cultures simply tells us that human rights are to be inferred from the reality of human nature.

Another way of justifying human rights comes from the tradition of the *social contract*. The existence of a stable and peaceable society depends upon its citizens agreeing to regulations that order life in a way that does the greatest justice to the interests of all. Thomas Hobbes, the English political philosopher, was one of the first to work out a rationale for this theory. The contract theory derives from the assumption that citizens fundamentally relate to one another as strangers, if not competitors. From such a perspective, society appears as a collection of individuals who, of necessity, must enter into a bargain to ensure their individual survival through providing for the survival of society.

In modern times, John Rawls has elaborated a theory of justice in terms of fairness that borrows from this tradition. In a thought experiment, Rawls asks us to suppose that we do not know how life is going to turn out for us. If we are then asked by what principle we would want life to be governed, so that we had the best chance, whatever our background, of leading a fulfilling life, we would automatically choose a system of fairness in which "all social primary goods – liberty and opportunity, income and wealth, and the bases of

---

[38] Messer, Neil, *Christian Ethics* (2006), London, SCM Press. If space allowed, it would be possible to expound the contribution that John Locke has made to the theory of natural rights. It should be noted that Locke, although he believed in the light of reason, never divorced it wholly from the revelation of God's will in the Bible.

self-respect – are to be distributed equally unless an unequal distribution of these goods is to the advantage of the least favoured."[39] We might call this 'the *reciprocal* theory': we should treat others in every respect as we expect to be treated. In essence, it is an argument from self-interest: in order for my rights to be honoured, I must, in all fairness, allow that the rights of others are equally observed.

A fourth way of justifying human rights comes from the tradition of utilitarianism. The argument states that, from observation, the implementation of human rights simply brings the greatest amount of human happiness to the greatest number. This apparently empirical conclusion might be termed 'the *consequentialist* theory' of human rights. Human rights' legislation clearly brings the best moral outcome for society. In practice, it has been shown that it limits human suffering most effectively, increases justice most comprehensively and enables people to choose their own destination in life most freely.

Objections to the language of rights

What makes us think that human beings possess rights? If a right is an entitlement to something deemed intrinsically good, such as the freedom to express oneself openly on any topic without the fear of arrest, imprisonment or even execution, who is supposed to be the agent that ensures that the entitlement is performed? In the case of civil and political rights, the responsibility lies, presumably, with a body that exercises a lawful authority to frame laws and another to see that they are implemented. However, this kind of discussion comes close to arguing in a circle, for the responsibility corresponds to the right and the right requires the responsibility. The initial question, then, is simply begged?

---

[39] Rawls, J. , *A Theory of Justice* (1971), p. 303, Cambridge, MA, Harvard University Press.

So, we are back with the enigma of tracing a credible source for the notion. The American Declaration of Independence (1776) suggests an answer:

> "We hold these truths to be self-evident, that all men are created equal, that they are endowed by their Creator with certain unalienable Rights, that among these are Life, Liberty and the pursuit of Happiness."

The source is the Creator who has, presumably, so ordered human life that every human being can claim certain dues or concessions that belong to that person by virtue of their humanity. The language of '*the* Creator' is, of course, the classical, orthodox language of the Christian creeds and other theistic religions. Its use makes a number of assumptions that are no longer consensual in the contemporary world; indeed, they would be disputed not only by secularists but by all adherents of non-theistic religions. Hence, in the form adopted by the *Universal Declaration*, the word Creator drops out:

> "All human beings are born free and equal in dignity and rights. They are endowed with reason and conscience and should act towards one another in a spirit of brotherhood." (Article 1).

The source of rights is no longer specified. The occurrence of rights is declared to be a fact; it is as though every human being is born into the world with two ears, two eyes, a nose, a mouth and rights. There are grave problems with this statement. The physical and mental characteristics of a human being are evident. Rights, however, comprise an abstraction; they constitute a theoretical entity. They do not exist simply by virtue of a dogmatic statement that they do so. Moreover, it is not self-evident that they exist. For large periods of human history, it has not been at all obvious that all human beings possess innate rights to life, liberty and the pursuit of happiness. Up to the beginning of the 19th century (a mere 200 years ago), slavery was considered a natural condition of human existence, and therefore justifiable. Many societies in the past have queried whether women are endowed with reason; at least with the same capacity as men. The claim to an inviolable, individual conscience is of recent historical appearance. It has been disputed (for example, in the case of conscientious objection to compulsory military service) even in so-called liberal societies, until well into the 20th century.

Alasdair MacIntyre opposes the notion of human rights on the grounds that there are no such things as self-evident truths. If I understand MacIntyre correctly, the recognition of a truth depends upon a prior commitment to a tradition of discourse in which the idea of truth makes sense. One such tradition, of course, is the Christian, which argues, precisely from a belief in the creation of the universe by a personal divine being, that there is a given reality made known not by some kind of universal intuition, but by the one who has created it. However, such a ground for a meaningful conversation about rights is not open to a non-theist, be he or she an evolutionary naturalist or religious monist.

A defence of human rights

Now, as MacIntyre and many others have recognised, the language of human rights makes sense within the framework of Judeo-Christian theism. For those who hold to a non-personal, accidental and purposeless origin to life, the concept of rights appears to be produced like a rabbit out of a hat. It is not even self-evident that the fundamental drive within nature is that of survival, so that survival might become a reason for inventing human rights.

There is a further problem, however, with postulating Judeo-Christian theism as an adequate basis for the concept of rights. The revelation on which it is based does not use this language. Nevertheless, with some credibility, Jewish and

Christian ethicists have deduced a notion of rights from the assertion at the end of the first creation narrative in the Bible that God made men and women in his image, blessed them and gave them certain responsibilities over the rest of his created order. Certainly, the *imago Dei* implies a unique status for human beings and equality between the sexes of universal extension. From these deductions, a firm belief in the essential dignity and value of all human beings is a legitimate inference. From the conviction that all that exists is the intentional result of the action of an entirely good and wise supreme being comes the belief that it is his will that the goodness and beauty of what he has created is protected and its destruction constrained.

In the biblical record, however, this protection is not couched in terms of rights, but of the imperative to do justice, to love kindness and to walk humbly in step with God.[40] This affirmation of the fundamental good for the whole of humankind is the principal charter for human behaviour. It is, however, quite distinct from the modern concept of human rights.

One of the problems for the human rights' hypothesis is that, within a secular framework, there is no reason to suppose that all people are either free or equal. The assertion that "all human beings are *born* free and equal in dignity and rights" (*UDHR*: Article 1) is a dogmatic statement that flies in the face of a mountain of contrary evidence. As such, it is a kind of whistling in the wind. It might be a goal to which humankind aspires, but it cannot be claimed as a reality. In a word, there is neither an ontological nor empirical basis for it. If, however, one were to say that "all human beings are *created* free and equal in dignity and rights," then there is a sufficient ground in the ultimate constitution of the world for freedom and equality to be considered an intrinsic element of what it means to be

---

[40] *The Book of the Prophet Micah*, chapter 6, verse 8.

human. Biblical faith simply does not think in categories of entitlement that somehow spring from those faculties (such as the capacity for logical reasoning or moral sensibility) that, supposedly, in the course of evolution, have marked out *homo sapiens* from the rest of sentient beings.

All that humans are and all that they possess is sheer gift. We happen to live in a universe that is shot through with gracious and generous acts of giving. The fundamental difference between being born and being created free and equal can best be seen in the way people think about the human status of those with severe mental disabilities and of the unborn child. The ontological reality of the *imago Dei* confirms such people as also unique human beings (apart from their actual features and attributes) to be afforded, therefore, every kind of protection and assistance.

The belief that human life is to be seen first and foremost as a gift from a wholly good God, and therefore to be protected from those who seek to deny the gift by rejecting equality and withholding freedoms, accounts for the granting of laws, which are designed to protect the status of human beings as the product of the divine act of creation. The law of the Lord springs from the consistently just and merciful nature of the Creator, who expresses, in his precepts, the requirements that have to be fulfilled for human beings to flourish as moral agents within a created order that is there as pure gift.

This is a far cry from a notion of human rights that can allegedly be read out of a nature that exists spontaneously, but aimlessly. The prophetic message that denounced the injustices of a ruling elite, who trampled the poor and vulnerable into the ground, did not stem from a general concern for human rights, though it would be evident that what was happening was unscrupulous exploitation, but because it took from them their means of livelihood and their equal participation in the community (both significant aspects of their being human).

So, every individual person, whatever their status in society, intellectual attainment or natural abilities, is equal with every other by virtue of their creation. God is no respecter of persons. There is absolutely no bias in his dealings with the men, women and children he has created. He acts towards all just as parents, at their best, treat their children; with equal affection and fairness.

The reality of creation is a powerful ground for dispelling every myth that some are born superior to others on the basis of race, ethnicity, nationality or gender, or acquire superiority according to their religious belief, ideology, educational achievements, occupation in life or financial success. The way in which Christian teaching has profoundly affected the whole question of human freedom, equality and rights in the pursuit of democratic principles of governance is, today, taken either as read, ignored or disputed. A little reflection, however, would demonstrate that there is no other basis:

"The fashion today is for rhetoric about human rights to ignore the need for any justification, let alone a theological one. It sometimes seems that human rights exist because people say they do. People matter because we choose to think that. We are equal because that is how we treat each other. The inadequacy of this should be clear. Rights then depend for their implementation on political agreements which may or may not last."[41]

The logical conclusion to be drawn from this discussion of the role of religion in public life is illuminating:

"How much should we rely on the theological justification? We can certainly ignore it, and hope that we can keep the superstructure without the historical foundation. That is probably not very feasible, and, in that case, we may have to change other beliefs about the importance of human

---

[41] Trigg, Roger (2007), *Religion in Public Life: Must Faith be Privatized?* p. 83, Oxford, OUP

beings, seeing, for example, no principled distinction between humans and animals. . .If we wish to retain our belief in the importance of humanity, and the 'sanctity' of human life, we may have to stress the role of religion in educational systems, and in the public sphere generally. So far from being privatized, it would turn out that religion was explicitly required to explain our intuitions about how society should be organized. To say that in the current Western world this is controversial would be an understatement."[42]

Conclusion

This presentation has argued that, despite all the rhetoric to the contrary, human rights are not self-evident. John Gray, in his book, *Two Faces of Liberalism*,[43] makes the perceptive observation that:

> "Rights are conclusions (arrived at by) long chains of reasoning based on core beliefs; *they are not foundations*" (my italics).

What he means is that the language of rights has come to be used as a way of protecting fundamental goods like justice, freedom and equality, but whose existence and justification must be based on a more primary bedrock. Otherwise, the discussion is circular: intrinsic respect for human beings is mandated because they possess inherent rights; rights are mandated because human beings are worthy of intrinsic respect. So, if rights exist, they do so only in consideration of a more basic reality.

Gray goes on to argue that in contemporary liberal societies rights language can be translated without remainder into that

---

[42] *Religion in Public Life*, p. 83.
[43] 2000, Cambridge, Polity Press.

of interests. When people use the term rights, with its high-sounding moral tone, in reality, they are talking about the particular interests of individuals and specific groups. This leads, he proposes, to the incoherence of the whole human rights discourse, because inevitably, interests clash:

"We are compelled to choose between rights because the interests they protect make incompatible claims...Often, no action that is open to us can avoid doing injury to some of them."

The consequence is that:

"Political philosophies in which rights are claimed to be fundamental pass over these conflicts of value. Yet, because they are endemic in political life, conflicts of value re-emerge in disputes over the rights we possess."[44]

So, if his reasoning is correct, the concept of rights begs a much more fundamental question. The issue is not that of rights, but what it is that makes a human being human. Every theory of rights comes back to this ultimate question, whether it is that based on natural law, contract, utilitarianism or the Kantian moral imperative. By observing ourselves and our biological and cultural history alone, we cannot determine a plausible answer. Every consideration that leaves out of account the claims of an extra-empirical reality to know the answer is doomed to frustration; it represents a reductionist anthropology and a relativist morality.[45] Michael Perry, an American law professor, draws the conclusion:

---

[44] *Two Faces of Liberalism*, pp. 84-85.

[45] In the latter case, Gray states that "there can be no definitive list of human rights. Rights are ...judgements about human interests whose content shifts over time as threats to human interests change," *Two Faces of*

"There is finally, no intelligible secular version of the idea of human rights; . . . the conviction that human beings are sacred is inescapably religious."[46]

However, even if Jeremy Bentham has been proved right in his conclusion that the concept of human rights is "a nonsense on stilts" (i.e. a highly exalted nonsense), and Alasdair MacIntyre in his insistence that the concept is a fiction, the question might still be asked; is it a useful nonsense or fiction? Given the inadequacy of any description of ethics that begins with the assumption of a closed-order material universe, does the notion of human rights nevertheless fulfil the aim, even if only in part, of protecting the equal dignity and sanctity of human beings; assuming that the latter are warranted truth claims on non-secular assumptions? It might be conceivable to assert that the current discourse on human rights is seriously flawed and yet to argue that dispensing with it altogether would be quite wrong, given that the idea can be built on a much firmer foundation than the secular one.

Given the reality of pluralist societies and their inability to find a credible reason for believing that human rights are somehow the natural outcome of the human condition, is this concept the best we can do? My tentative conclusion is that, however we may answer, not to take the concept for granted, but to call it into question, opens up possibilities for fresh thinking in what is proving to be an ethical minefield. There is an alternative discourse. It begins with the notion that all human beings, without exception, are to be treated as possessing totally equal value, *because they bear, whether they acknowledge it or not, the image of their creator.* This God, the alternative affirms, requires his creatures to promote and

---

Liberalism, p. 113. In his view, if there are such things as universal rights, they only remain so for a limited time, according to circumstances.

[46] *The Idea of Human Rights: Four Inquiries*, (1998), p. 35, Oxford, Oxford University Press.

protect the ontological, inviolable status of all humans as sacrosanct. Every human being is accountable to one who will judge them on the criterion of whether they have protected the singular significance of every other human as a sacred trust. Even were this alternate belief to lack substantial evidence, which it does not, it would at least supply a proper basis for the use of human rights' language.

Select bibliography

Clapham, Andrew, (2007), *Human Rights: A Very Short Introduction*, Oxford, OUP

Donnelly, Jack, (2013/3), *Universal Human Rights in Theory and Practice,* Ithaca, Cornell, University Press

Douzans, Costas and Gearty, Conor (ed.), (2014), *The Meanings of Rights: The Philosophy and Social Theory of Human Rights,* Cambridge, CUP

Freeman, Michael, (2011/2), *Human Rights: An Interdisciplinary Approach,* Cambridge, Polity Press

Glahn, Benjamin, Amon, Anver M., Ellis, Mark S., (2012), *Islamic Law and International Human Rights Law*, Oxford, OUP

Griffin, James, (2008), *On Human Rights*, Oxford, OUP

Holder, Cindy and Reidy, David (eds.), (2013), *Human Rights: The Hard Questions*, Cambridge, CUP

Hopgood, Stephen, (2013), *The End Times of Human Rights*, Ithaca, Cornell University Press

Hunt, Lynn, (2007), *Inventing Human Rights: A History*, New York, W. W. Norton

Moyn, Samuel, (2014), *Human Rights and the Uses of History*, New York, Verso

Ruston, Roger, (2004), *Human Rights and the Image of God*, London, SCM Press

Salih, Jaradat, (2014), *Human Rights in Islam: A Comprehensive and Comparative Perspective*, Lambert Academic Publishing

Stackhouse, Max L., (1984), *Creeds, Society and Human Rights: A Study in Three Cultures*, Grand Rapids, MI, Eerdmans

CHAPTER 6

Liberal, progressive and radical

"We are in a sort of terminological haze in which the meaning of words is so variable that one no longer knows exactly what the discourse (is) about. . ." (Tariq Ramadan)

"Liberals can understand everything but people who don't understand them." (Lenny Bruce)

Introduction

When trying to sort out the immense variety of meanings given to these three associated adjectives, so freely scattered about in public discussion and private conversation, Ramadan's conclusion appears to be self-evident. In each case, as we shall consider, the words have been, and are, used with almost opposite interpretations, according to the perspective of the person who employs them, or the context in which they appear. Moreover, their meaning has shifted markedly over the course of time. Thus, the original ideal that was expressed some centuries ago has often been turned on its head in contemporary thinking.

The diversity and shift of usage raises the question as to whether the words have any stable currency in modern usage, or whether they have lost all symbolic significance and have become quite arbitrary signs utilised in the sense of pure personal preference. To attempt any kind of analysis that might possibly lead to a little clarification of words so loosely construed is probably a thankless task that will result in being shot at from all directions. These three words are used by people with strong convictions about moral issues and identity politics and are guarded jealously as representing, in their opinion, the pinnacle of forward thinking. In reality, as adjectives, they are all too often attached to concepts, ideas, ideals, programmes, policies, procedures and practices in radically (yes!) different ways.

If this is so, and my research has thrown up plenty of evidence of the diversity and contradictory nature of the way the words are used, should one draw the conclusion that there is so much confusion that the words no longer serve any useful purpose? Or, is there some merit in trying, at least, to indicate how the meaning of the words is being stretched to such an extent that the same word has come to indicate conflicting opinions? It would be foolish to attempt to adjudicate between different meanings in a way that would achieve a consensus. It might, however, prove worthwhile to point out how these particular words demonstrate an abuse of language and are used as examples of abusive language.

When people come to expropriate language for particular partisan causes, communication becomes ambiguous, misleading or even insincere. The rhetoric may sound auspicious, but it breaks down, when the conversation partner has little idea what the other is talking about. The exchange of views becomes, then, a kind of slanging match, in which one throws in, at regular intervals, these words, their equivalents, or their conventional opposites, to cover over the lack of a coherent argument. Reasoning together requires at least a minimal agreement on what a person intends when they employ certain words and phrases. To the contrary, dialogue is nothing more than a 'war' of words, in which each side is trying to use language to outmanoeuvre the other and secure a knock-out blow. If anyone thinks I exaggerate, just look at many of the responses to any internet blog that expounds a particularly controversial opinion on any important topic.

Unfortunately, the philosopher Wittgenstein's dictum that the meaning of language is determined by its usage breaks down in the case of each of these three words. The etymology of the words can only help to a certain degree, for modern linguistic libertarians insist that language is continually changing. However, if there is no common, agreed meaning, then we are back to personal inclination. If that is what people want, so be it. I still believe there is some virtue in attempting to create acceptable boundaries, so that we all still have a chance of understanding one another, and therefore agreeing, or agreeing to disagree, about substantial inter-human concerns and disputes.

Liberal

The linguistic background to the word can give some guidance as to how it should be used. It is derived from the Latin *liberalis*, meaning free. Its prime meaning stems from the cluster of words that give expression to the idea of liberality, such as generous, open-handed and bountiful. It suggests a person who is unstinting in their willingness to give from the resources they own.

From the context of material giving, it has been transposed to that of the moral life. Thus, liberal has come to infer the advocacy of an individual's freedom of action and expression, being broad-minded and easy-going about a person's lifestyle choices. A liberal upbringing implies a family where the children are accorded plenty of discretion in terms of behaviour, rules are kept to a minimum, risks are taken and ample personal preferences allowed. The opposite stance would be narrow-mindedness, dogmatism, inflexibility or strictness.

In social terms, liberal has come to mean freedom from rules, regulations and constraints imposed either by cultural convention or legislation, from past traditions considered outmoded and from inherited privileges. In recent years, a liberal attitude has led to the liberalisation of laws on Sunday trading, gambling, abortion, divorce, and same-sex relations, in the sense that former moral absolutes have been discarded and the legal system that enshrined them considerably relaxed.

In the political sphere, liberal infers a maximum protection of civil liberties, open and transparent government, minimum of state interference in people's personal lives, a disinclination to impose a collective morality on the populace and an openness to reform. It also means a firm commitment to democratic ideals, such as the rule of law, checks and balances to the centralisation of power, a free press, a mature and dependable opposition to current government and actions taken with the consent of the governed. A democratic society which is functioning well is also one where people not only recognise quickly when legitimate freedoms are being curtailed, but are able swiftly to put the matter right. Such a society will have in place mechanisms of scrutiny, information, participation and accountability.

In economic life, liberal has usually indicated a minimal regulation of the market. Freedom in the market place embodies a number of interlocking liberties: the individual ownership of property and the right to dispose of it, according to personal determination, the possibility of unfettered bargaining between employer and employee concerning the price value of labour, the ability to transfer capital assets across national boundaries, the maximising of net income across the population in order to stimulate economic growth through consumer choice (and, therefore, a minimal regime of taxation) and the desirability of letting the market determine research projects.

The liberal tradition, then, advocates a minimal state, an open society and the priority of the individual. Given the tendency towards autocratic government, in which small groups of people assume the right, on the basis of an alleged superior vantage point, to govern in the best interests of all, the genuine liberal believes it is best to err on the side of the protection of the individual, even if, consequently, some social injustices are not rectified.

The origins of modern liberal thinking and policies are linked to the English Revolution of 1688 and the political philosophy of John Locke, which later profoundly influenced the founders of the American state. His theory of the right to the basic values of life, liberty and property is based on the notion of self-evident truths, given in natural law and known in experience. These basic rights, written into the constitution of the universe (by God in Locke's thought) were inalienable. No other person, and certainly not collectives, like governments, had any prerogative to disregard or annul these rights. No individual should be forced to place his life, liberty or property at the disposal of another. Freedoms are not conferred on individuals by the will of a sovereign state. Consequently, they cannot be removed by any authority. They are bestowed by the very fact of being human and they take precedence over all other legal codes and practices.

Utilitarianism

Subsequent off-shoots of the liberal tradition modified, to some extent, the original vision. In the thinking of utilitarians, a good in society is brought about by creating the maximum amount of happiness for the maximum number of people, whilst not diminishing happiness for anyone. It assumes that everyone desires happiness, or the gaining of pleasure, as their chief end. It also assumes that, when the greatest degree of happiness is being achieved for everyone, the individual's own happiness will be increased. The outcome of this view is that everyone should enjoy the freedom to pursue optimum happiness, as they conceive this, as long as they do not curtail the same pursuit for everyone else.

Such a theory has ended up in a consequentialist ethic, where good and bad actions are judged solely by their out-comes. All actions are permitted, as long as they do not cause harm. Despite the fact that they are deeply flawed as adequate accounts of how to arrive at ethical values, utilitarianism and consequentialism enjoy enormous popularity in contemporary Western cultures, because they favour individualism and freedom of expression.

Happiness, however, is too vague a notion to count for much in ethical terms. If, for example, abusing others makes a person happy, it should not, for that reason, be tolerated. And it should not be tolerated since it is intrinsically wrong, not because it contradicts another person's pursuit of happiness. The notion of happiness begs the question about what is legitimate, or illegitimate, to pursue. It implies some notion of the good. This must be decided on grounds much more basic than that the good is what makes the individual happy.

Then again, consequences often cannot be predicted with any degree of accuracy. Moreover, notions of good and evil must be brought into play prior to judging whether the consequences of actions are acceptable, or not. Consequences cannot determine the nature of good and evil. Rather, their desirability, or wrongness, is judged by an intrinsic understanding of the latter.

Libertarianism

As a political and philosophical ideal, libertarianism extends the liberal tradition to what some think is its logical conclusion. They may agree that minimal government is necessary to avoid anarchy: people need to be protected from the evil intents of others; contracts freely undertaken between two parties need to be upheld and enforced, and the nation's security needs to be protected from the threat of subversion from within and attack from without. These commitments imply taxation in order to pay for a police force, a system of law and the military. However, libertarians are extremely reluctant to go beyond these minimal requirements. In particular, they would question the raising of taxes to pay for a welfare system. Human beings, it is argued, flourish when they are given economic freedoms to pursue their own self-interests and are held responsible for their own situation in life, irrespective of the circumstances into which they were born.

Libertarianism promotes a philosophy of free enterprise, in which individuals are encouraged to advance their own self-improvement by becoming self-reliant; creating wealth through unrestricted competition and saving some of it for a 'rainy day'. Libertarians tend to argue that welfare systems incline towards being *over-protective*, thereby contributing to a *paternalistic,* dependency syndrome, through making decisions on others' behalf, thereby undermining further their self-confidence, and having a limited *rectifying function* by merely enabling people to keep going. Social welfare, it is argued, rarely addresses adequately long-term problems, such as motivation, self-belief and a full recovery from abuse and neglect.

A shift of meaning

As we have seen, being liberal used to mean advocating the maximum freedom possible for individuals in their private lives and in the way they conducted their economic affairs, consonant with an equivalent freedom for all other individuals. Liberals tended to believe in minimum sanctions against violations of the law, restorative justice rather than exemplary punishment and belief in the power of education to correct anti-social behaviour, prejudices and the pursuit of economic self-interest.

Liberals are inclined to believe in the essential goodness of human nature and that the right incentives will always bring out the best of human characteristics. Where individuals fail to achieve their potential or mess up their lives by following destructive practices, liberals are prone to believe that external factors are the main causes: such as bad parenting, disruptive family life, bullying at school, poverty and discrimination. Change the circumstances and you will change the person.

In recent years, people, glad to be known as liberals, have probably become less optimistic, more sceptical about the limitless ability of human ingenuity to overcome obstacles. Now they tend to support an increasing amount of legislation to tackle what appear to be endemic problems of interpersonal violence, distrust, the exploitation of vulnerable people and deprivation. The state is increasingly called upon to intervene in the attempt to roll back the effects of mistaken choices or sheer wickedness, rather than try to tackle the underlying reasons why the choices were made, or the wickedness indulged in the first place. Harmful eating habits, unhealthy lifestyles, disruptive work-life balances, no fault divorces and cruelty to children are creating a situation where the health and social services of a nation are being put under intolerable strain. All legislation can do is pick up the pieces and attempt to stem the tide of self-indulgence, self-harm and the abuse of power.

Liberals hold two contradictory beliefs simultaneously: the conviction that people have a right to follow their particular preferences in life without officious interference by others, but, when their choices result in trouble or tragedy, the state is called on to ameliorate the consequences. The belief that misfortune is basically due to personally uncontrollable outside conditions leads to the conclusion that sufferers are usually the victims of unjust, discriminatory or exploitative circumstances.

The problem with this perspective is that it generates a kind of sentimentality on the part of the fortunate, who treat the alleged victims as a class of people, rather than see them as individual subjects responsible, in many respects, for their own situation. Emotions are elicited by an image and an ideology which is reluctant to hold people accountable for their own choices. To talk of responsibility, blame and guilt in connection to a person's predicament is considered slanderous, hurtful and damaging to their self-esteem.

The likely causes of failure become hidden; they are not recognised, and therefore cannot be dealt with. The best help that a person struggling to overcome their problems may receive is the encouragement to face honestly the degree to which they are self-inflicted and advice about how they may set their life on an even path again. Liberalism used to signify individual liberty, with the individual responsibility that freedom entails. In more recent times, it has come to embrace state paternalism; a kind of ambulance service like the one that picks up patients and takes them to the nearest Accident and Emergency unit.

Assessment

Liberal thought, despite the failure, in many instances, to come to terms with real people, has advocated genuinely liberating beliefs and policies. Freedom of thought, expression and action is a fundamental good over against the natural tendency in human affairs to concentrate and solidify power in the hands of the few and to control the thinking and activities of the many. Taking seriously the autonomy of the individual over against the power of the collective (state, government, family, ethnic group, religion, ideology and tradition) is a desirable corrective to enforced conformity. A certain freedom in the market place from bureaucratic controls for initiatives and creativity is a welcome alternative to a state-run planned economy that suffocates or prevents individual inventiveness and enterprise.

All well and good; but only to a point. Liberal thought has failed to take seriously enough the moral ambiguity deeply etched into human nature. In other words, it is too naïve about the perfectibility of the human being. The fathers of modern psychoanalysis (Freud and Jung) recognised that the main evidence for our flawed human nature comes in our unwillingness to admit our deeply ingrained defects. Jung put it this way: "The jungle is in us, in our unconscious. . .The human mind carefully refrains from looking into itself."[47] Liberals have

---

[47] Jung, C.G. (1976), *Jung Letters,* Vol. II, p. 608, London, Routledge and Keegan Paul, quoted in Marsh, John (2012), *The Liberal Delusion: The Roots of our Current Moral Crisis*, p. 16, Bury St. Edmunds, Arena Books.

tended to accept the Enlightenment myth of the 'noble savage', innocent until the ravages of degenerate outside influences have corrupted them. The theory of primal virtue does not explain the origin of evil. If people are corrupted by external forces, who started the ball rolling? Evil is not an abstract entity for which no one has responsibility; it is a real presence, the result of human perverseness.

All in all, the language of liberal should be used with caution. There is enough evidence to show that its connotations are ambiguous. Therefore, it cannot be used to claim the moral high ground in any controversy about moral signposts or legislative policies. Its present construct may be doing damage to its original intention.

Progressive

By and large, a person who advocates liberal ideals is also likely to think of themselves as progressive in their attitudes towards the past, present and future. Linguistically, progress is derived from the Latin noun *progressus* (from the verb *progredi*) meaning an advance – *pro* (forward) and *gradi* (walk). In other words, it signifies a forward movement. In its etymological sense, it does not have to mean anything more than a movement in the direction in which a person is going. If one is on a hike, with a destination in view, and stops for a rest and refreshments, resuming the walk is to make progress towards the intended goal. However, if the hike is a circular one, so that one eventually returns to the place one set out, it is still possible to say that one has made progress throughout the walk, by covering new ground, even though one finishes up where one began.

The illustration is important because, for reasons that will become clear, a huge amount of intellectual and emotional energy has been invested in the notion of progress, often without realising the ambiguity and pitfalls of the concept. In ordinary, everyday parlance, progress is used to highlight a positive and admirable outlook on life. To be progressive is to favour reform that leads to improvements in personal and social wellbeing. It is to advocate liberal ideas and new and experimental enterprises. It suggests an overridingly optimistic interest in the future: associated words would be *developed*, *evolved*, *forward*, *advanced* and *latest*. It evokes notions like contemporary, enlightened, cutting-edge, space-age, avant-garde, go-ahead and ultramodern. Progress is considered to imply movement from a lower to a higher stage of human development, one which is superior to, and therefore more beneficial than, that which has gone before. It indicates a situation in which a particular way of thinking or mode of operation has been superseded and replaced by one which is more acceptable, commendable, auspicious and worthy.

Naturally, progressive is contrasted with notions that represent its opposite. Not to progress is either to stand still or to go backwards. In the case of the hike, people who, before reaching the half-way point, have become exhausted by the energy expended and decide to turn around and go back have failed to make any further progress. They regress. In their attitude to change, they are considered reactionary, die-hard in their beliefs, traditional, cautious, hidebound and conventional. They are stuck in the past, fearful of change, defenders of the *status quo*, not willing to move with the times. In other words, generally speaking, they hold back the onward march of history.

Progressivism as a philosophy

The idea that human endeavour is on an upward curve, forever climbing to a higher plateau, is the legacy of a Judeo-Christian view of history. Human life has been set free from the endless repetitions of the yearly cycle of nature, in which everything returns to where it began. Left to themselves, pagan religions, which hallow the eternal recurrence of all life, would never have broken free from a circular or cyclical view of existence.[48]

The whole idea of progress was given an enormous stimulus by the Enlightenment. The beginning of the Industrial Revolution promised immense improvements to the quality of life of the general populace through a continuous control of the forces of nature. The expansion of empirical knowledge would help people understand much better natural processes, thus contributing to the overcoming of ignorance, superstitions, and illusions. A new understanding of the power of reason would vanquish dependence on the delusions of religious belief, which acted as a break on free thinking. Powerful intellectual forces were combining with the new discoveries of science to create a powerful surge away from the dead hand of the past towards the more sunlit uplands of the future. Ideas of liberty, democracy and modernisation were in the air. A new continent across the Atlantic was being opened up, dynastic autocracies were being demolished and new constitutions framed.

It appeared to these pioneers that they had discovered a pattern, or law of history, that consisted of irreversible changes in societies in one direction only; that of improvement. This belief was given an immense boost by the dialectical philosophy of Hegel, followed by Karl Marx. Hegel believed that history, through the dissonant interaction of opposing ideas and material forces, gradually revealed an upward movement towards an absolute Ideal; the reconciliation of human life away from its various alienations. Marx built on Hegel's dialectic pattern, using his concept of the negation:

---

[48] The substance of this view is expounded, amongst others, by Lasch, Christopher (1991), *The True and Only Heaven: Progress and its Critics*, New York, W.W. Norton; Wright, Ronald (2006), *A Short History of Progress*, Edinburgh, Canongate Books; Gray, John (in various books, including *The Silence of Animals: On Progress and other Modern Myths*, (2014), Harmondsworth, Penguin Books).

"For Hegel, the dialectic method proceeds by means of eliminating the self-contradiction of two contrary categories by means of negating the original negation. . .For Marx the category is the original social arrangement within its specific historical moment. . .In Marx's thought the historical movement of the negation is advancing inexorably towards its final resolution in what he called 'the realm of freedom'. . .Marx appears to think that the intrinsic forces of technological advance, engendered by the new successes in science and by human labour, once reconciled again to its proper object through the negation of the exploitative action of capitalist accumulation, will produce a qualitatively different kind of society."[49]

Many others believed in a universal law of social development. The inner logic of society was progress. The 19th and 20th centuries have indeed witnessed significant signs of progress in many different areas: the end of the legitimising of slavery, a rise in rates of literacy, a gradual increase in equality between the sexes, the reform of penal institutions, the amelioration of harsh and cruel punishments often for minor offences, a decline of absolute destitution, a general rise in living standards and conditions of life, a lessening of the gruelling nature of labour, an extension of life-expectancy and an increase in leisure time. Then there is a whole shift of attitudes towards the non-toleration of poverty, hunger, inadequate shelter, lack of education, the subjugation of women, inequalities, racial bigotry, complemented by a growth of humanitarian sentiment in the concern for social justice and the overcoming of violence in all its forms.

Progressivism as an idealistic philosophy or ideology has been the subject of many interpretations. A recurring theme among historians has been the belief that the notion of progress

---

[49] *The Future of Reason*, pp. 144-145.

as a worthy goal to be pursued has become the secular substitution of belief in divine providence and the promise of a new heaven and a new earth. In other words, progress makes no sense, unless there is a strong conviction that "this vale of tears" will be transformed, that history will not end in annihilation and nothingness, but will be redeemed and recreated as a kingdom of exemplary justice, peace and reconciliation, in which suffering, exploitation, hate and violence will be replaced by healing, compassion, love and gentleness. This is the vision promised by the Hebrew prophets and the early Christians and carried forward in numerous millenarian and utopian dreams down the ages. For progress to have any traction, this aspiration for substantial change for the better has to continue to inspire peoples and nations.

It may be that the Judeo-Christian faith has inculcated a firm belief in a sequence of time that is moving towards a destiny that, in many respects, reverses the hitherto experience of life on earth. It may be that this faith has challenged and largely displaced the rival belief in a cyclical view of life that has no meaningful beginning or end. However, the faith has never suggested that human beings on their own, in their own strength, by their own wisdom, can ever achieve this promised land. Indeed, because the proposition of a new earth, created by human hands alone, has time and again produced its opposite (such as the gulag, killing fields, gas chambers, the caliphate), an increasing scepticism about the vision has arisen.

Christianity, which has been the dominant creed in European history for sixteen centuries, is now accused of misleading humanity by insisting that human history will have a righteous end. However, it is not the fault of the religion. The actual message is much more nuanced. On the one hand, there is an expectation of a whole new creation in which only righteousness and goodness will be present. On the other hand, and in accordance with present experience of a corrupted existence, there will be a massive judgement on all the evil and sin that has been committed since the beginning of the human race. This is not a human judgement, carried out according to the twisted views of justice proposed by totalitarian regimes, but a divine verdict based on a perfect view of good and evil.

A fundamental misunderstanding of the Christian hope has led some people to decry the whole notion of a linear view of history and the attempt to remake the world, and to advocate a return to the cyclical rhythm of nature. In other words, these people believe that the over-hyped language of progress has wrought more damage than it has brought benefits. After the most vicious century that the world has probably ever known, now is the time to be less ambitious and much more circumspect. Change, when it introduces genuine improvements in living conditions, is to be welcomed, but without all the baggage of pretending that, overall, the world is a better place to live in. History, they assert, is not on an upward path to the celestial fields; nor, by and large, is it deteriorating and slipping back into the Dark Ages. History is simply the record of the achievements and follies of flawed human beings. It is the chronicle of successes and failures, nothing more and nothing less. Above all, history simply repeats itself.

Progressive means whatever you wish

The word sounds good. In technologically advanced societies, where innovation and novelty are highly praised, nobody wishes to be considered out of touch with or unappreciative of the latest ideas and experiments. To be considered progressive is to be in the vanguard of new exploratory ventures and cutting-edge research. To resist moving out to the frontiers of fresh thinking and bold, creative enterprises is to be left behind by history, to be stuck in old-fashioned, out-dated, superseded projects, or so the language would indicate. Let me attempt to illustrate, with two quite different examples, the way this language is manipulated by people with specific agendas they wish to push. To call them progressive is to rouse expectations, gather an audience, set a mood, predispose a positive response, be on the side of the next generation. It is hard to kick against the pricks of the next fashion.

The first example is 'progressive education.' Our concern here is not to explore, in depth, the merits or defects of what goes by this name. That would require a quite different kind of analysis. Our interest is in the way the language around the notion is operated. So, in the literature advocating progressive education, we find a whole set of buzz words. Learning is a process, more than a journey to a destination. It is wholistic, i.e. attending to the needs of the whole pupil. It is learning from one another in community, where competition and individual comparisons are deliberately avoided. Motivation to learn is intrinsic, i.e. it arises from within the person concerned; not for the sake of gaining qualifications that will boost job prospects, but for the love of discovery and the widening of horizons.

Education is a life-long process; it begins by instilling in the pupil a desire to think, read about and question the world in which they live. It nourishes curiosity, creativity and a critical mind. Students are challenged to think deeply about issues, constructing and testing their own ideas by becoming independent of conventional wisdom. It is learning through the active participation of the learner; so, young people are invited to take part in designing the curriculum. The goal of education is to prepare people to take responsibility for their lives, attend to the needs of others, abide by democratic principles of decision-making. Discipline is to be self-imposed through the process of reasoning to the child's best interests.

Now, many of these practices are admirable, for they respect the human integrity of the individual. However, they are largely based on an optimistic view of human nature. On the other side of the debate, what is termed 'traditional education' is said to be based on a pessimistic view of a young person's ability to respond to the challenge of self-motivated learning. And, if one has bought into the whole ideology of progress, it is a sin to be negative about the 'infinite' potential of every person to be captivated by the endless fascination of a world with always more features to be explored.

So, the flip side to a progressive education is a traditional, conventional, well-established, time-honoured education (note the language!). This kind of education is based on an inflexible curriculum, imposed on schools by government. Education is seen as what is done to children. It is based on rewards and punishments. Discipline is exercised on the basis of the negative consequences of stepping out of line. Learning achievements are assessed through regular homework, tests and grading. Examinations based on memorisation are considered the acid test of a pupil's educational performance. Bench-marking, i.e. comparison with national grade averages or that of similar schools, is deemed to be a sure sign of the quality of teaching. Learning is the passive absorption of information, deemed necessary by remote political authorities for the good of the nation struggling to prosper in a highly competitive world.

Above all, the goal of education is to enable students to fit into the competitive job market of advanced capitalist economic systems. This means either acquiring a university degree (preferably in a subject regarded as being useful to the economy – for example, engineering, medicine, computer sciences, mathematics, business studies, technological design, languages) or joining a recognised 'vocational' training course that leads to employable qualifications. The emphasis of this approach to education is on linguistic and mathematical abilities. When it comes to filling in job application forms and undergoing interviews, the capacity to articulate skilfully one's own language, both in written form and verbally, is of crucial importance.

These two quite distinct approaches to education may seem like caricatures. Perhaps, to make the point, they are, to some extent. The main concern that can be deduced from this con-centration on the type of language that is wheeled out in support of particular educational theories is that, in each case, the assumptions are not being properly examined. It is the power of language alone that captivates or repels the imagination. Most people, in advanced liberal democracies, would like to think of themselves as progressive, for to be categorised as traditional is to be reactionary, belonging to a past generation, defenders of the *status quo*, antiquated, and so on.

The second example, briefly, is that of a self-styled 'progressive Christianity.' The 'Progressive Christianity Network', on its website, defines itself thus:

"Members of the PCN seek a *credible* and *inclusive* way to follow Jesus. We are unafraid to question *traditional* church teaching; we value *contemporary* thought and *recent* biblical understanding. We do not offer *a set of answers*, but we invite you to join us in *asking questions*."

I have emphasised the words in italics in the hope that the reader can see the way that language is manipulated in the interests of a particular programme of thought. There is no critical reflection on how they are being used. Each of them is highly loaded, to make an impression. These sentences represent, perhaps, a typical collage of expressions designed to maximise an impact recognisable as progressive; but, never mind the content! What is *credible*, on what basis, and who decides? (No answer). What is progressive about being *inclusive*? How is this distinguishable, if it is intended to be, from a thoroughgoing relativism? (No answer). People, who do not call themselves unequivocally progressive, also question some traditional teachings. However, they manage to do this without getting rid of the baby with the bath water. What is so special about *contemporary* and *recent*, unless one has already accepted the priority of being progressive? Finally, how does one know what questions to raise, without a minimum of convictions taken to be answers? (No answer). Perhaps, the question is, what is so virtuous about being progressive? One assumes that the PCN has a set answer to this, otherwise its objective "melts into thin air" (to borrow a phrase from Karl Marx and Friedrich Engels). What we encounter in this vision of progressive is the liberal (primary sense) use of ambiguous words in order to clarify a particular version of an ambiguous word. The result is a pretty meaningless statement.

A critique of progressivism

There are a number of reasons why the notion of progress has come under critical scrutiny, not least in the thinking of those who call themselves post-modernists. Some say that it is a necessary antidote to despair, as to give up hope for a better future is to induce disillusionment. In other words, it is a kind of whistling in the wind to keep up the spirits. If faith in the future is removed, motivation to work with others for an improving world is lost. Human beings will tend to fulfil the old precept, "let us eat, drink and be merry, for tomorrow we die." What vision is left for which it is worth sacrificing individual goals?

Those who believe in progress tend to portray history in a one-sided way, ignoring or minimising the failure of civilisations to live up to their early promises. The reality is that humankind is not marching anywhere. Writers such as Oswald Spengler,[50] taking a sober, non-romantic view of human history, find a consistent pattern of advance and decline in all societies. One might say that people with a similar outlook on human exploits to his are inclined to a 'cup half-empty' theory of the achievements of civilisations of the past and present. Those who take a 'cup half-full' view have been deluded by the astonishing advances in technological achievements and, in the nations of the West and pockets of elites elsewhere, the extraordinary growth of material prosperity.

---

[50] *The Decline of the West: Vols. 1 and 2*, (2013), Windham Press.

Science tends to be touted as the great mechanism for overcoming massive problems confronting the present generation: such as, climate change, new strains of virus resistant to anti-biotics, poverty and ageing populations. However, it is totally impotent to solve the problem of human moral deficiencies and indifference to spiritual realities. Ronald Wright comments that:

"We no longer give much thought to moral progress – a prime concern of earlier times – except to assume that it goes hand in hand with the material. Civilized people, we tend to think, not only smell better but behave better than barbarians and savages. This notion has trouble standing up in the court of history."

Later, he observes,

"The Roman circus, the Aztec sacrifices, the Inquisition bonfires, the Nazi death camps – all have been the work of highly civilized societies. In the twentieth century alone, at least 100 million people, mostly civilians, died in wars. Savages have done no worse. At the gates of the Colosseum and the concentration camp, we have no choice but to abandon hope that civilization is, in itself, a guarantor of moral progress."[51]

Nevertheless, he remains moderately optimistic about the future. Likening civilisation to a great ship steaming at speed into the future, he says:

"We may not be able to foresee every reef and hazard, but by reading her compass bearing and headway, by understanding her design, her safety record, and the

---

[51] *A Short History of Progress*, pp. 4, 33-34.

abilities of her crew, we can, I think, plot a wise course between the narrows and bergs looming ahead."[52]

Evidence suggests that progress, like evolution, can be regressive. Improvements are not necessarily cumulative; they can become more irrational. In our haste to promote change, we often do not foresee unintended consequences, and of course change is not the equivalent of progress. John Gray, in his book *Heresies: Against Progress and Other Illusions*,[53] may be unduly pessimistic about the whole discourse on progress, but he is also realistic. He writes that:

"in science progress is a fact, in ethics and politics it is a superstition. . . (It is an illusion to believe) that it (scientific knowledge) can affect any fundamental alteration in the human condition. . .Science merely enlarges human power, it does not make it more reasonable or peaceful, or help remake the world."

Echoing the Genesis narrative of the fall of humanity, he concludes that:

"knowledge does not make us free; knowledge can be a sin."

Compared with the immediate post-war period (1945-1960), subsequent decades in the Western world have 'progressively' created a fundamental moral deficit by removing traditional solutions to what are at bottom fundamental spiritual disorders, inducing all kinds of anxieties and neuroses. In the frenetic search for more knowledge, we have put information in its place and abandoned wisdom.

---

[52] *A Short History of Progress*, p. 3.
[53] 2004, pp. 2-6, London, Granta Books.

Radical

If ever there was a word whose meaning is so variable that it is difficult to find any consistency in its use, it is radical. Radical is indiscriminately used, for example, of Islam and of Feminism. In the first case, it is used of groups who interpret the Qur'an and the hadith to advocate extreme ways of taking power, imposing political control over nations, and introducing the rigours of Islamic Sharia law. In the second case, it is used of groups who advocate the end of patriarchal structures of power in society, the equalisation of opportunities, benefits and responsibilities between men and women, and a thorough educational programme designed to eradicate all traces of machismo among boys and men. Radical Islam subjugates women, denying them access to education, insisting that they cover themselves completely in public, thus denying them their individuality and person-hood, and consigns them to the role of child-bearing and domestic servitude (think Taliban, Islamic State, Boko Haram). Radical Feminism seeks to liberate women from the conventional roles that have been imposed on them by male-dominated societies, to recognise in practice their equal humanity and the gifts and skills they can offer for the good of society. How, then, can the same word be used of two such contrasting groups of people with wholly divergent aims and objectives?

It appears, from the numerous other examples that could be given, that the term radical, when applied to beliefs, opinions, political, social and religious movements and groups of people, is used indiscriminately. Its introduction into the field of politics is usually ascribed to Charles James Fox, a British politician, who served briefly two terms as Foreign Secretary in 1782-1783 and 1806. In 1797, he is said to have declared for a 'radical' reform of the voting system to expand the franchise to all male citizens. Radical, in this context, presumably means profound changes to the political order. By extension, it came to denote parties that advocated far-reaching reforms in social and political matters.

Usually, it has been applied to political movements supporting 'left-wing,' socialist policies. In this sense, the radical wing in politics is impatient with gradual reform measures. Rather, it champions changes that pull up existing systems by the roots, in order to establish new plants in the place of the old. However, it is also applied to programmes of change inspired by contrasting political and social philosophies. Especially in the USA, radical is applied to extreme conservative ideals – a minimal state, a significant lessening of regulations on businesses, an increase in obstacles to the withdrawal of labour (the right to strike), the free flow of capital across borders, a low tax regime and minimum spending on state-sponsored social security systems. These proposals characterise the 'radical right.'

Certain right-wing parties might merit the epithet radical, in so far as they seek to undermine the power hegemony of traditional parties by offering substantial changes in the way that politics is conducted. They might, for example, advocate an end to confrontational politics, in which opposition parties not elected to government see themselves duty bound to counter any policy put forward by its rival. The smaller parties often stand on a platform determined to scrutinise, challenge and reform the system of privileges enjoyed by parliamentarians, senior civil servants and the countless unelected advisers and consultants employed by politicians of all the main parties. They will usually stand on a manifesto pledged to root out corruption (of those parties used to exercising political power).

In Britain, the United Kingdom Independent Party, when first established, sought to fulfil a role in representing those who find that they are disenfranchised by the traditional political class. It seemed to appeal to those who, broadly speaking, may be called 'the left behind': those whose views on life do not resonate with the leadership of the traditional parties. The latter belong to certain sectors of the privileged and socially liberal middle-classes: they are highly educated (often through independent schools and the 'elite' universities); they are comfortable in an ethnically and culturally diverse society, not having to live alongside recent immigrants; they are well-travelled; cosmopolitan; financially in one of the top brackets of earners; disconnected from the lives of those who, for example, are not as well-educated or qualified – the unemployed, people marginalised on the outer estates of the large urban conurbations, who lack the contacts and skills that enable them to gain advantages in society. UKIP identified itself with those who see multiculturalism as a means of fragmenting British society, a threat, intensified by the acceptance by default of unrestrained immigration, to an integrated core British cultural identity, built on a consensus of values hammered out by generations of British people whose ancestors have lived in the islands for hundreds of years.[54]

It is not the purpose of this book to make judgements on either the 'radical left' or the 'radical right', but to point out the seeming anomaly of using the same adjective to describe political ideologies that appear to be at the opposite ends of a spectrum. It calls into question the usefulness of using the word at all. And yet, people do use it and apply it to all sorts of causes, just because it possesses a certain rhetorical resonance. So, in general, radical is not being used in a kind of neutral way of any belief or course of action based on strong convictions and extreme principles, whatever those convictions

---

[54] For a contemporary assessment of the motives that drive those associated with UKIP, see Ford, Robert and Goodwin, Matthew (2014), *Revolt on the Right: Explaining Support for the Radical Right in Britain*, Abingdon, Routledge. I want to clarify that I, personally, am not an enthusiastic supporter of UKIP or any party that advocates political policies generally identified as being right-wing. I actually believe that to talk glibly about right-wing and left-wing political groups is yet another example of the abuse of language. Following the end of the military dictatorship in Argentina in the early 1980s, a new party was formed that declared itself to advocate policies of the 'radical centre.' Perhaps this was intended as a joke; it certainly showed the meaninglessness of using the term radical.

or principles may be; rather, it is used to reinforce a cause that should be approved, admired and applauded.

Thus, the 'radical' feminist is not just a feminist, but one who believes her views and campaigns are the most forthright and uncompromising in the struggle to eliminate patriarchy from the body politic. She may even criticise and rebuke others in the 'sisterhood' who are satisfied with small gains in the struggle for recognition and equal treatment, pressing the movement not to make concessions until all its demands are met. Likewise, radical Islamists are not just committed Muslim believers, who seek to live out the specific directives of their religion in their private life, but those who believe it is their responsibility to work for a world-wide Islamic order that implements Sharia law over the whole of society, and to accomplish this, where necessary, by force. The radical Muslim sharply divides the world into 'true believers', 'apostates' and 'unbelievers' (or kafirs), and has absorbed an ethic of the end justifying the means (suicide bombing, terrorist attacks, all-out war, the slaughter of anyone (whether combatants or not) who refuses to interpret Islam as they do).

So, radical is simply employed as a weapon of approval for the group with which one identifies. Max Haiven and Alex Khasnabish state that the most powerful meaning of radical stems from:

> "the Latin *radix* or root in the sense that radical ideas, ideologies or perspectives are informed by understanding that social, political, economic and cultural problems are outcomes of deeply-rooted tensions, contradictions, power-imbalances and forms of oppression and exploitation. Radical means reforms must be based on and aimed at transformation of fundamental qualities and tenets of the system itself."[55]

---

[55] *The Radical Imagination: Social movement in the age of austerity,* (2014), London, Zed Books, p. 8.

This definition suggests that radical must be understood, not so much as a return to the roots of a belief or situation, but the *uprooting* of any opinion or programme of action that anyone wishes to interpret as being conservative, traditional and moderate. However, the authors go on to say, significantly:

"The idea of radicalism cannot be monopolised by any point on the political spectrum."

The conclusion seems to imply that, actually, to deem anything radical is simply a reaction to that which is deplored. Thus, we come to a situation where radicals are ultimately reactionaries, because their response to a belief or situation they do not tolerate is largely a reflex. The excessive and misplaced use of the term has rendered it largely meaningless; it has become a redundant epithet as, for example, in the titles of books like: *Radical Contentment: The Power of Enough; Radical Gardening: Politics, Idealism and Rebellion in the Garden; Tales for Little Rebels: A Collection of Radical Children's Literature*. The latter title gives the game away. The sub-title should read *A Collection of Radical Literature for Children*, seeing that using radical to describe children (7-11 year-olds?) does not make much sense. The self-styled radicals are the adults writing stories with a certain twist, intended presumably, from the first part of the title, to make them into rebels.

In one Thesaurus I use, some of the equivalent meanings given to the term radical are basic, fundamental, intrinsic and deep-seated. Not one gives the impression that it would serve as an emotive, high-sounding, declamatory piece of rhetoric. That, often, seems to be the main intention of calling anything radical.

Conclusion

I hope that the survey and analysis of the use of these three words has shown that either they mean very little, they are highly ambiguous, or they can be used in ways that contradict the intention of those most attracted to them. They are abused words, because they are not employed with distinct and carefully constructed meanings, but to be used in ideological power games. They insinuate a mood that resonates with a certain spirit of the age. When repeated often enough, they take on a certain potency and intensity that defies rational engagement; they by-pass critical examination, appealing often to prejudice, misrepresentation and misinformation, as if the mere pronouncement of the word *liberal, progressive* or *radical* were sufficient to conclude a discussion with the ace of trumps.

Select bibliography

Ford, Robert and Goodwin, Matthew, (2014), *Revolt on the Right: Explaining Support for the Radical Right in Britain*, Abingdon, Routledge

Gray, John, (2004), *Heresies: Against Progress and Other Illusions*, London, Granta Books

Gray, John, (2014), *The Silence of Animals: On Progress and Other Modern Myths*, Harmondsworth, Penguin Books

Hamid, Rawfik, (2008), *Inside Jihad: Understanding and Confronting Radical Islam*, self-published

Lasch, Christopher, (1991), *The True and Only Heaven: Progress and its Critics*, New York, W. W. Norton

Lakoff, George, (2002/2), *Moral Politics: How Liberals and Conservatives Think*, Chicago, University of Chicago Press

Marsh, John, (2012), Articles: 'Liberalism', 'Libertarianism' in *The Liberal Delusion: The Roots of our Current Moral Crisis* Bury St Edmunds, Arena Books

Miller, David (ed.), (1991/2), Articles: 'Liberalism', 'Libertarianism' in *The Blackwell Encyclopaedia of Political Thought*, Oxford, Blackwell

Minogue, Kenneth, (2006), *The Liberal Mind: The Psychological Causes of Political Madness*, St Charles, IL, Free World Books

Nawaz, Maajad, (2012), *Radical: My Journey from Islamist Extremism to a Democratic Awakening*, London, WH Allen

Ramadan, Tariq, (2009), *Radical Reform: Islamic Ethics and Liberation*, Oxford, OUP

Trilling, Lionel, (1950), *The Liberal Imagination*, New York, New York Review of Books

Turner, Rachel S., (2008), *Neo-Liberal Ideology: History, Concepts and Policies*, Edinburgh, Edinburgh University Press

Wright, Ronald, *(2006), A Short History of Progress*, Edinburgh, Canongate Books

CHAPTER 7

Fundamentalism

"Clearly, the term fundamentalism has become a word used to accuse the other. (A) 'fundamentalist' is always the other. When one refers to oneself, be it referring to one's religious, political or economic views, one always prefers to use the term 'radical'." (Leonardo Boff)

"Fundamentalism is a word of abuse levelled by liberals and Enlightenment rationalists against any group, religious or otherwise, that dares to challenge the absolutism of a post-Enlightenment outlook." (Malise Ruthven)

"In public debates and everyday conversation, the term 'fundamentalism' is used widely simply to name persons or attitudes we do not like." (Torkel Brekke)

Preliminary remarks

After researching into the subject of its use and abuse, I am tempted to conclude either that there is no such thing as fundamentalism or, more likely, we are all fundamentalists, particularly those who so self-righteously attack it. As hinted at in the quotations above, unravelling its meaning is fraught with problems.

Firstly, there is a distinct lack of consensus on how one should define the concept. Sometimes it is used of any movement that appears to have retreated into a kind of conceptual or institutional citadel, unwilling to face and grapple with change in society. However, at other times, it is used to signify groups that advocate the transformation of concepts and institutions. A return to fundamentals can mean either a regress to the doctrinaire certainties of another age or a re-evaluation of the basis on which thought and action is coherent, consistent and purposeful.

Secondly, contradictory statements are made about the main features of fundamentalist opinions. What, for example, is the attitude of alleged fundamentalists to the age of modernity? Is it supportive of scientific research and the discoveries that it makes? Is it enthusiastic about technological advances that flow from the research? Or, if science comes up with conclusions that apparently contradict cherished religious or ideological beliefs, is it denigrated by those who hold them? It has been accused of being too much wedded to a kind of positivist use of scientific methodology, but also of being highly sceptical of some results flowing from the scientific enterprise. It has been condemned as being intellectually simplistic, favouring dogmatic convictions, even when they appear to fly in the face of carefully produced empirical evidence. On the other hand, it has also been charged with being over intellectualist (almost rationalistic) in its regard for careful scholarship. It has been characterised as being pre-eminently theoretical and conceptual, keen to show that it is on the side of credible scholarship, and yet, at the same time, adversely judged as appealing mainly to the emotional realities of alienation, exclusion, fear, helplessness and a sense of loss.

Thirdly, all too often, the word is used prejudicially. Many critics – sometimes called the 'metropolitan commentariat' (self-styled purveyors of what is acceptable to believe) – are belligerent towards what they describe as fundamentalisms. Indeed, the word itself is designed to inculcate a feeling of negativity: a disdain for infantile beliefs and immature actions. These critics, however, appear to lack understanding of and empathy towards beliefs they condemn as fundamentalist.

They sometimes border on the paranoid in their treatment of the subject. The term is almost uniformly used in a pejorative sense to apply to people who are reactionary, authoritarian, unreasonable, literalist, and anti-modern. Bhiku Parekh says that it is used as:

> "a polemical hand-grenade to be thrown at those we detest and fear and whom we wish to fight and defeat with a clear conscience."[56]

Some people assert that fundamentalists still live in the 'dark ages', from which enlightened people have fortunately become free. The former represent an unliberated past; the latter represent their liberated future.

On the other side of the controversy, there are not many people who would describe themselves as fundamentalists, as this term has come to be identified. Most of the literature on the subject has been written by those who viscerally detest what they take to be fundamentalist beliefs and inspired actions. It is hard, therefore, to find a cogent defence of the word, except when applied in the strict sense of the conviction that there exist fundamental principles guiding action, without which communities would fall apart. In that sense, everyone is a fundamentalist, since, in practice, no one is a consistent relativist.

The Origin of the term

There seem to be two historical moments in which fundamentalism has come to the fore. It was first used of a particular trend in American Protestantism at the turn of the 20th century, which, in the face of modern and liberal adaptations of Christian faith, sought to re-emphasise what its leaders

---

[56] *The Concept of Fundamentalism*, (1991), Peepal Tree Press.

considered to be the non-negotiable fundamentals of Biblical faith. Between 1910-1915, a series of books called *The Fundamentals: A Testimony of Truth,* was published in twelve volumes by scholars associated with Princeton Theological Seminary, New Jersey. It became a symbolic reference-point and label for the fundamentalist movement.

The essential truths of the Christian faith were identified as follows:

(a) The *inerrancy* of the Bible. It is free from all error in all that it positively affirms, not only in the areas of doctrine and morals, but also history and the empirical world. Whatever the Bible says without ambiguity and uncertainty cannot be false.

(b) The *deity* of Jesus. The statement on Jesus Christ made at the fourth Ecumenical Council of Chalcedon, particularly the virgin birth, is an accurate statement of the reality of who he is. As a consequence, any belief that implies that he *became* the Son of God by some process of adoption is false. He was and is the pre-existent second person of the Trinity, sharing all the attributes of the Godhead.

(c) *Substitutionary atonement.* Jesus suffered on a Roman cross to pay the penalty for the sin of the whole of humankind, past, present and future. He died in the place of every individual human being to avert the just judgement of God on their sinfulness.

(d) *Physical resurrection.* The Jesus who died on the cross was raised to new life in bodily form. The Jesus who appeared to his disciples during a period of forty days after his resurrection was the same Jesus, albeit with a transformed body, who had died, been buried and remained in a tomb for three days. The resurrection was not a new awareness of the presence of Jesus, subjectively understood, nor a change of perception in the outlook of his disciples; it was an encounter with a man of flesh.

(e) The *second coming* of Jesus. Jesus will physically return to this world in space and time, not as a mystical experience, but as a person.

All these fundamentals are non-negotiable. They are the test of orthodox, historic, mainstream Christianity. There can be no room for alternative psychological or spiritualising interpretations. The identity of faith itself is at stake. Therefore, it is legitimate to break communion with any who have reinterpreted basic core beliefs in any way that denies their plain sense.

The actual term, 'fundamentalist', was coined by a Baptist leader, Curtis Lee Laws, in 1920. In an edition of the Northern Baptist periodical in the USA, *The Watchman Examiner*, he described himself and other evangelicals as militants willing to do "battle royal" to preserve the "fundamentals of Christian faith" from evolutionists and biblical critics who, at the time, were infecting mainline seminaries and colleges.

In the 1970s, the term fundamentalism re-emerged, attached, in particular, to two growing phenomena. Firstly, the religious right in the USA re-emerged, led by people such as Gerry Falwell, a spokesperson for the 'Moral Majority,' and Pat Robertson, one of the pioneers of the 'electronic church.' They were deeply conservative in both their theology and their political alliances. Both reflected and stimulated a mood across the country that brought Ronald Reagan to power in the early 1980s. Secondly, Islamic 'extremism' became a more powerful force on the world scene with the success of the Iranian revolution in 1979 that brought the Ayatollah Khomenei to power. These trends were paralleled by other religious groups: such as a nationalistic version of Hinduism in India (the Rashtriya Svayamsevak Sangh), of Buddhism in Sri Lanka, of certain Jewish factions in Israel (such as the Haredim and the Gush Emunim) and various sects and cults. What all these organisations are said to have in common is a rigorous, literalistic and selective interpretation of their respective holy books.

In recent years the word has become increasingly attached to certain expressions of Islam: much publicised movements such as Al-Qaeda and Jamaat-e-Islami and political parties like Hamas (in Palestine) and Hizbullah (in the Lebanon). Even more recently, its use has been consistently applied to uncompromisingly harsh militant groups fighting the Assad regime in Syria like Islamic State, Boko Harem in Northern Nigeria and Al-Shabab in Somalia.

Definitions of the term

These have been varied and numerous. A long research undertaking, centred on the University of Chicago, called, 'The Fundamentalist Project', describes fundamentalism as an approach and set of strategies by which beleaguered believers attempt to preserve their distinctive identity as people or as groups by the selective retrieval of doctrines, beliefs and practices from a sacred past.

Others have defined fundamentalists as militant or radical religious groups opposed to modernity and secularism which seek, in the words of the Library of Congress Catalogue, "a revival of orthodox or conservative religious beliefs and practices," or religious sectarians, who see their principle task to be the defence of the faith against external enemies. These are the 'true believers', who attempt to arrest the erosion of religious influence in society, fortify the religious boundaries of their communities and create viable alternatives to secular institutions and behaviour.

One author, Torkel Brekke,[57] argues that fundamentalisms should be defined as a specific kind of reaction to the erosion of authority in public and private life in the modern world. As a global phenomenon, it is, for him, more about religious

---

[57] In his book, *Fundamentalism: Prophecy and Protest in an Age of Protest,* (2012), Cambridge, CUP.

authority and styles of religious leadership than specific doctrines that fundamentalists attack or defend.

Features of fundamentalism

Most commentators agree that fundamentalism is a response to some of the characteristics and values of a post-Enlightenment society. It has been described by James Barr as "a new form of faith, that did not exist until modern times."[58] It may be understood by looking at five defining attitudes.

Firstly, the attitude to *knowledge*. In terms of its explicit or implicit philosophical underpinning, it would be considered 'foundationalist'. This is taken to mean that fundamentalists believe that they have direct access to indisputable truth, about which there cannot be any doubt. This leads to a supreme confidence that God is on the side of those who oppose all forms of untruth. Truth is at hand to those who look for it in the right place. It is a gift to be received from the one author of all truth. One may be certain that one can know the truth without ambiguities or confusions. The possessor of the truth about the universe, life and death is then in a position to proclaim it to all without compromise. In some versions, fundamentalist groups seek to impose their 'true' beliefs on communities and societies, either by being elected to office (for example, the fairly recent case of the Muslim Brotherhood in Egypt) or through violence (for example, The Taliban and ISIS).

Secondly, the Fundamentalists' attitude to their *foundation documents*, be these the Bible, the Hindu holy books, the Qur'an, the Book of Mormon or other writings, it is alleged, tend to interpret their sacred scriptures literally. They do not allow much room for the idea of a progressive revelation or for the contextual appropriateness of the message they announce. Not only the text has to be inerrant, their interpretation of it

---

[58] Barr, James (2010), *Fundamentalism*, London, SCM Press.

must be the only legitimate one. New readings of the text are seen as threatening. There is a great reluctance to be corrected by other interpretations. Those fellow-believers who step out of line are denounced as apostates, heretics, heterodox or revisionists.

Thirdly, the attitude to *culture*. Fundamentalists, on the whole, are pessimistic about the ability of societies to overcome problems and defects. They support theories of disintegration and would tend to be sceptical of any notion of inevitable progress, as outlined in the previous chapter. They endorse the evidence that modern and post-modern cultures are infused with a spirit of relativism and pluralism that leads to civil disorder and moral confusion.

The mission of religions is to rescue society from its extreme moral indifference. In order to achieve this, the first task is to ensure that religious communities remain pure, i.e. that they live by norms that are basically counter-cultural as interpreted by the communities' leadership. Thus, for example, in the USA, groups that have been identified as fundamentalist may be very strict about drinking habits and sex before marriage and yet support the gun lobby's stance on the right to own and carry fire-arms in public.

Fourthly, the attitude to *political life*. Fundamentalists, of the kind we have been describing, tend to get involved in public life in order to get liberal laws changed. The aim is to return society to godly values, identified with a traditional social order. These values encompass principally the reversal of an intense individualism, exemplified in the proliferation of human-rights' claims, the subordinate place of women and girls in society, a strong disciplinary ethos in the nurturing of children, rigorous punishment for crime (including capital punishment), a strong emphasis on individual responsibility and an interpretation of poverty that finds its main cause in cultural and personal dispositions.

In its religious manifestation, those referred to as funda-mentalists are inclined, primarily, to single out co-religionists as the main object of their wrath and indignation. In the USA, liberal and progressive Christians are condemned for supporting the right of women to choose the abortion of their pre-born child and homosexuals and lesbians to live together as married partners. In the case of Muslim zealots, they castigate those Muslims who are prepared to live peacefully under secular or semi-secular regimes, especially if these hold power in Muslim-majority countries. They tend to blame what they see as the weak state of Islam in the world on the failure of the majority of Muslims to live by the strict standards of traditional, codified Islamic law.

Fifthly, the attitude to a *pluralist* society. Fundamentalism has been characterised as a reaction to the shock of encountering the 'Other,' especially when the 'Other' holds views and engages in activities essentially incompatible with the Fundamentalists' own. The idea that there may be many different paths to salvation or numerous legitimate lifestyles is a particular cause of distress and abhorrence. The Fundamentalist, in this understanding, is then temperamentally opposed to religious toleration, especially when the religions in question support the liberalising of laws on such matters as abortion, marriage and divorce, same-sex regulations, transgenderism and euthanasia.

Varieties of Fundamentalism

Christian

There are a number of movements, organisations and groups that are popularly described as being fundamentalist. We have noted some of the more celebrated examples that have come to the fore within the last fifty years or so. The term originated among North American Protestants in the first two decades of the 20th century. Their focus was on protecting and preserving the core beliefs of mainstream Christianity against what they considered to be the revisionist tendencies of other

Christians who desired to reinterpret the faith to make it more accommodating to a rationalistic and morally 'enlightened' world-view. The disputes that were engendered then, and to a certain extent are still current today, were largely to do with the authority and interpretation of the Bible, and the place of tradition and reason in deciding what constitutes authentic Christian teaching and practice.

At a considerably later stage, Christian fundamentalism became associated with Christian groups (particularly in the USA) that espoused a certain political agenda: scepticism towards the long-term benefits of a welfare state; opposition to a nation-wide health service funded through taxation; strong doubt about development aid being the main answer to poverty in underdeveloped countries, and promotion of the so-called 'American Dream' of hard work, initiative, innovation and entrepreneurship as the real solution to endemic destitution, wherever found. They are nationalists with a strong conviction that the US has been given a 'manifest destiny' to spread its form of the rule of law, democracy, moral integrity and economic freedom for the pursuit of wealth-creation. All these goods, they are convinced, come from spiritual and moral principles that originated in the religious convictions of the 16th century reformers, refined by subsequent generations of Protestant believers, and enshrined in the founding documents of the new nation in the 18th century.

Jewish

The manifestation of fundamentalism within Judaism has taken a rather different form. For some interpreters it centres on religious Zionism, that is the powerful conviction that a parcel of land at the East end of the Mediterranean belongs, as an eternal gift of God, to the physical descendants of Abraham, Isaac and Jacob. These, then, have a divine right to settle this piece of land as their own property, irrespective of who else may, by aeons of possession, already occupy the land. Using an argument similar to that advanced by some of the early European settlers in North America, their claim on the land was justified by their aspiration and ability, using modern agricultural methods, to use the land productively.[59] The slogan 'a people without a land for a land without a people,' in spite of its highly questionable accuracy, became a powerful inducement for Jews to return to what was once their homeland.

For other interpreters, Jewish fundamentalism is seen most clearly in Haredi Judaism, a form of ultra-orthodox faith practised by Hasidic sects who reject most manifestations of modern, secular cultures – television, the internet, secular newspapers and books. They wear distinctive dress, impose a rigid separation of the sexes, and are assiduous in performing the rites prescribed in traditional law. Paradoxically, they are opposed to the state of Israel, partly on the grounds that it is a self-proclaimed secular state, and partly because they believe that only the Messiah, when he comes, can recreate the nation and restore it to its pristine state.

Muslim

Fundamentalist is an adjective which, especially since the atrocities of 9/11 in the USA, is applied in the 21st century most readily to certain Islamic movements and groups. Such an ascription is contested. Certainly, one of the manifestations is the internal dispute within Islam about the relationship of its teaching to contemporary secular cultures. One of the main issues is the question of how much reinterpretation of its holy book, the Qur'an, of the traditions of the sayings and practices of Muhammad (the *hadith* and the *sunna*), of the codification

---

[59] The assertion was given some theological backing in the 17th century by John Locke. His argument is summarised in Northcott, Michael *An Angel Directs the Storm: Apocalyptic Religion and American Empire*, (2007), p. 48, London, SCM Press.

of its teachings in systems of law is allowable, to take into account changing social, cultural and political realities.[60] Islamic fundamentalism is often linked to a desire to reinstate the Caliphate, to institute Sharia law in place of Western-influenced jurisprudence, to reverse the promotion of women's rights, as understood in the West, to oppose fiercely and violently the freedom of religion, conscience and speech, and to eliminate the kind of democracy that has its origin in the West – the right of all citizens to manifest their political choices not only through secret ballots, but also through referenda, protest, lobbying and the work of independent, non-governmental organisations.

Family resemblances?

Due to the frequency with which the word fundamentalist is applied to what, on the surface, appear to be quite different phenomena, a dispute has arisen amongst commentators about whether there are enough common features across the various religious manifestations for the term to be used meaningfully of a world-wide, collective reality. There is a secondary question concerning the justification of using the same language of views and practices that do not have a direct religious attachment.

The answer to the first question probably depends on how precise a definition is required for the attribution to have any meaningful content. As the quotes at the beginning of the chapter show, the word is easily abused as a derogatory term for beliefs and actions which intellectually and emotionally certain sectors of society find beyond the pale. It is undoubtedly, and perhaps usually, used as a word of abuse. The basic issue is whether the word stands for a set of beliefs and principles

---

[60] I explore these questions in Kirk, J. Andrew (2011), *Civilisations in Conflict? Islam, the West and Christian Faith*, Oxford, Regnum Books International.

that cannot be described by using any other term. Does it add something novel to a reality that no other description captures to the same extent?

Malise Ruthven[61] points out that the term exists on the borders of a semantic field, straying into other words like extremism, sectarianism, doctrinairism and ideological purism. None of these alternative concepts, however, are any more illuminating, as they are primarily used with a subjective, idiosyncratic sense. Fundamentalism cannot be equated with primitivism – a return to medieval thinking – or restorationism – the rehabilitation of some supposed 'golden age' of the past (for example, Muhammad's rule in Medina) – or an ultra-conservatism. All these expressions beg many further questions.

Fundamentalism only acquires a fruitful meaning when compared to something which is not fundamentalist. It has been pointed out that all orthodox Muslims are, in the strict original meaning of the word, fundamentalists, as they hold that every word in the Qur'an has been transmitted, sentence by sentence, from God through the mediation of an angelic messenger, memorised by Muhammad and later written down accurately, word for word. This view of the very text of the holy book goes beyond the way in which even the most orthodox Christians view the nature of the Bible.

Florian Pohl,[62] disputes the generalised use of the word across different religions on the grounds that it is premised on an Enlightenment understanding of religion, namely as a distinct sphere of life kept separate from other spheres such as politics, economy, law and education. This, he argues, is a

---

[61] *Fundamentalism: A Very Short Introduction*, (2007/2), Oxford, OUP.

[62] In his chapter for the symposium, Wood, Simon A. and Watt, David Harrington (eds.), (2014), *Fundamentalism: Perspectives on a Contested History*, Columbia, SC, University of South Carolina Press. In a recent book, Armstrong, Karen, *Fields of Blood: Religion and the History of Violence,* (2014), London, Bodley Head, also objects to the minimalist, reductionist understanding of religion, prevalent in secular discourse.

product of culture; it cannot be universalised. This assumption, he goes on to assert, undermines the ability to distinguish the different ways in which religions function in public. It also leads to a secular society's deeply felt need to regulate and relegate religion purely to the private realm of individual piety. What religion is up to, then, particularly in the Muslim world, is viewed as a deviation from what ought to be normal and befitting in the modern world.

Despite these diverse reasons for treating the term fundamentalist with extreme caution in view of its lack of specificity, there are plenty of authors who insist that there is still sufficient evidence of a family likeness to be able to speak coherently of one phenomenon. Perhaps, in its essence, however acquired, its core reference is to the self-confidence that some people have, in the face of uncertainties, confusion, anxieties and traumatic events in the world and their own circumstances, in the reality of absolute truth, their ability to discern it and their duty to propagate it.

Is it a useful convention to use the term fundamentalist outside of the religious context to which it has been normally attached? Commentators are divided over the issue. Probably, the majority think that employing the word of certain beliefs and attitudes held by people who profess no religious creed widens its application beyond what is helpful. It increases the probability that it is simply being used as a catch-all phrase to chastise regressive views that others find unacceptable. Ruthven, for example, believes that the use of the word in a non-religious framework is not analytically useful. If it is true that fundamentalists are partly defined by their rejection of a secular world-view and many of the moral consequences of a secular social ethos, it would seem contradictory to accuse certain secularists of fundamentalist traits.

On the other hand, its use in the context of particular ideologies has become more frequent in recent years. Leonardo Boff, for example, a Brazilian liberation theologian, believes it is justifiable to accuse people who hold to specific economic and political opinions of being fundamentalist.[63] Defenders of an extreme form of laissez-faire capitalism, for example, might fall into this category. Conversely, promoters of state-controlled economies might also be put in the same bracket. He defines a fundamentalist as one who confers an absolute status on their own point of view and is resolutely intolerant of competing viewpoints. Such an understanding could fit, equally, a devotee of an entirely self-regulating market economy or an advocate of a centralised, command economy.

Finally, Alister and Joanna McGrath seek to turn the tables decisively against some contemporary atheists in their critique of religious fundamentalists:

> "A total dogmatic conviction of the correctness which pervades some sections of Western atheism today. . . immediately aligns it with a religious fundamentalism which refuses to allow its ideas to be examined or challenged."

In particular, they castigate Richard Dawkins, in the aftermath of the publication of his book *The God Delusion*, for displaying some of the same characteristics that the latter reserves for religious people:

> "Dawkins is resistant to the calibration of his own certainties, seeing them as being luminously true, requiring no defence. He is so convinced that his own views are right that he could not bring himself to believe that the evidence might legitimate any other options – above all, religious options."[64]

---

[63] See, *Fundamentalism, Terrorism and the Future of Humanity,* (2006), London, SPCK.

[64] *The Dawkins Delusion? Atheist Fundamentalism and the Denial of the Divine,* (2007), London, SPCK.

If the McGraths are correct in their depiction of the way some contemporary atheists use highly contentious, polemical arguments, often based on dogmatic, inaccurate descriptions of religious beliefs, to dismiss all opinions that contradict their own, they may have a point. If religious fundamentalists are guilty of refusing to come to terms with a pluralist society, believing that secular world-views should be eradicated from public discourse, because they are harmful to human flourishing, then the 'new atheists', seem to have a similar attitude and agenda, although in reverse.

Evaluation

If one holds to 'liberal' and 'progressive' ideals, fundamentalism will be seen in a predominantly negative light. Indeed, as has been implied in the preceding discussion several times, fundamentalist becomes a short-hand for all opinions, programmes, policies and ideals that are incompatible with a self-selected, enlightened and emancipated stance on social and cultural issues. In order to be balanced in our assessment, we might well ask whether there are any redeeming features. Does it possess any strengths to offset, in part, its weaknesses?

In my opinion, it is right about emphasising *the importance of truth*. The reality of the truth question cannot be evaded. It confronts the anaemic tolerance, in the name of freedom of choice and non-discrimination, of perversions of all kinds that lead ultimately to the self-destructive path of an excessive individualism. It exposes relativism as an intellectual sham and a practical impossibility, that is, a view of life that cannot be consistently lived out in the real world. It challenges secular humanism in its tendency to have a superficial and reductionist understanding of reality and the place of human beings within it.

By inference, it shows that everyone is committed, in practice, to foundational beliefs, even when theoretically denied by ingenious (and ingenuous) philosophical arguments. It unmasks the dogmatisms of those who proclaim their broad-mindedness. Perhaps, part of the hostility towards fundamentalism by those who assume their intellectual sophistication and superiority is that it exposes their 'shadow self,' that is, the self that suppresses the doubts in their own mind about the validity of their own belief-system. It raises the nagging question, therefore, whether it is possible to believe in anything without being a 'fundamentalist'.

On the other hand, certain strands of fundamentalism have great weaknesses. Fundamentalists appear unable to distinguish between absolute and provisional certainty about truth, between the reality of its existence and a total grasp of its content. They do not appear very ready to accept correction. There is an unwillingness, on the part of religious devotees, to admit the complexity implicit in understanding sacred writings of the distant past and distinguishing between the message of the books and their interpretation.

There is an equal unwillingness on the part of 'ideological fundamentalists' to admit that certain ideas, be they Marxist, Socialist or Capitalist, can be open to probing critiques by people who do not have any vested interests in the theories and practices they are critically evaluating. Some commentators refuse to countenance any truth claim that cannot be substantiated by strict empirical methods of research and confirmation. They reduce knowledge of reality to what can be demonstrated by the experimental methods of the exact sciences. This approach could also be considered a form of fundamentalism, for its insistence on only one possible source of knowledge.

However, if the 'solid rock' of the fundamentals is not to degenerate into 'sinking sand,' beliefs about the rock have to be as solid as the rock itself. The only way that such beliefs could be established is by declaring them infallible, and thus denying that any other option but the ones I, or the group I adhere to, have affirmed possible. Fundamentalists, then, are obliged to identify their beliefs, moral values and political standpoints either with the will of God, or a particular explanation of historical forces, or self-evident truths. They tend, then, to present themselves as spokespeople for the one and only, final, absolute creed that should be accepted.

Fundamentalists tend to be blind to the distinction between justifiable beliefs and practices and cultural values and institutional norms: the example of the veiling of women in some Muslims' understanding of what their faith requires is one of the most prominent. There seems to be a strong correlation between a resilient religious orthodoxy and conservative political stances, resulting often in an uncritical nationalism and a strong antipathy to 'left-wing' views. Likewise, 'avant-garde' political philosophies, no less dogmatic, appear to be wholly irreconcilable with 'right-wing' views.

Do not these realities have much more to do with certain positions taken as the result of peer-group pressures than to a rigorous analysis of the opinions put forward for espousing particular moral values and political stances? To categorise political tendencies 'left-wing' or 'right-wing,' and consequently, depending on one's viewpoint, unaccept-able, may well be a substitute for careful, rational assessment of the strengths and weaknesses of what those tendencies stand for.

In the last analysis, as we have suspected all along, everyone who holds an opinion, whether religious or non-religious, with sufficient vigour and lack of compromise, and is willing to act on it, is a fundamentalist. If this is so, then the use of the word is superfluous, meaningless and unhelpful.

T.S. Eliot, in his poem, *Burnt Norton*, might have been referring to the terminological inexactitude of the use of fundamentalism when he wrote:

"Words strain, crack and sometimes break, under the burden, under the tension, slip, slide, perish, decay with imprecision, will not stop in place, will not stay still."

Select bibliography

Almond, Gabriel A., Appleby, R. Scott and Sivan, Emmanuel, (2003), *Strong Religion: The Rise of Fundamentalisms Around the World*, Chicago, University of Chicago Press

Armstrong, Karen, (2001), *The Battle for God: Fundamentalism in Judaism, Christianity and Islam*, London, William Collins

Brekke, Torkel, (2012), *Fundamentalism: Prophecy and Protest in an Age of Protest* Cambridge, CUP

Bruce, Steve, (2000), *Fundamentalism*, Cambridge, Polity Press

Harris, Harriet A., (1998), *Fundamentalism and Evangelicalism*, Oxford, OUP

Herriot, Peter, (2007), *Religious Fundamentalism and Social Identity*, Hove, Routledge

Lumbard, Joseph E.B., (2009), *Islam, Fundamentalism and the Betrayal of Tradition*, Bloomington, World Wisdom

McGrath, Alister and Joanna, (2007), *The Dawkins' Delusion? Atheist Fundamentalism and the Denial of the Divine*, London, SPCK

Rahman, Fazlur, (2000), *Revival and Reform in Islam*, Oxford, One World

Ruthven, Malise, (2007/2), *Fundamentalism: A Very Short Introduction* (Oxford: OUP

Wood, Simon A. and Watt, David Harrington (eds.), (2014), *Perspectives on a Contested History*, Columbia, SC, University of South Carolina Press

CHAPTER 8

Homophobia

"I now think that human beings use words as tools to create particular sexualities as specific kinds of phenomena, and that the reality of a particular kind of sexuality is dependent on and inseparable from the different words we use socially to describe it ...Human beings use words to create particular perceptions of the world, on which they then act, and alter the social institutions around them." (Jonathan Katz, *The Invention of Heterosexuality*)

Preliminary Remarks

Of all the words chosen because of their ambiguity and the way in which they are misunderstood and misused, homophobia is probably the most outstanding. It is also the most controversial. A huge amount of political, social, cultural and moral energy is poured into the use of the word. In general terms, homophobia is commonly employed in ordinary speech (the media, surveys, reports, websites and other means of communication) to refer to every suggestion of disapproval of homosexual behaviour.

The accusation of homophobia, in what has become its conventional use, is intended to signal a strong negative reaction to this disapproval. In other words, it is applied indiscriminately to any conversation, discourse, piece of research, point of view or action critical of the current pro-homosexual agenda, whose policies we will discuss in the course of this chapter.

One of a number of tragic consequences of the present debate concerning the social and moral positioning of homosexuality within communities is the almost complete lack of serious and composed engagement with the real live issues. Unfortunately, the term homophobia (or homophobic) is often used as a weapon to disrupt or end a potentially fruitful discussion between people who take very different views of homosexuality's many aspects. Such a strategy, in the interests of silencing those who oppose some of the changes that have taken place in the perception and defence of homosexual conduct, does not address the concerns, but simply forces them underground. In particular, the recourse to law and litigation is especially counter-productive, because the outcome is dependent, not so much on the strength of rational argumentation and well-researched evidence, but on the preconceptions of law-makers, interpreters and enforcers.

In my opinion, what is needed is a sincere and honest conversation between people who passionately hold divergent views, for the benefit of acceptable accommodations and, yes, toleration, in the sense of allowing opposing opinions to be expressed and acted on in a civilised manner. The rhetoric of homophobia (and the associated language of prejudice, bigotry, narrow-mindedness and discrimination), used loosely and indiscriminately, mostly harms the cause of those who wish to promote the acceptability of homosexual lifestyles. Those accused of being homophobic, when they have genuine cause for concern about the rapid acquisition of homosexual rights without proper democratic consultation and sober debate, will not go away. They are likely to continue to press for their contrary rights to be acknowledged and respected and may be prepared to engage in civil disobedience to attain reasonable adjustments in representation and legislation.

The main purposes of this chapter are, then, to consider carefully the way in which the language of homophobia is being used to the detriment of civil accordance and the common good, the reasons why its use is so prevalent and how the situation could be changed to secure greater social harmony around this highly contentious and disputed controversy. Above all, it is intended to appeal to honesty in assessing evidence and responding to reasoned argument. Jumping to mistaken conclusions, stereotyping, ridiculing or dogmatising will not do: they simply demonstrate the paucity of the arguments of those who resort to such tactics.

Understanding the meaning of homophobia

Before considering the standard dictionary definitions of homophobia, it is important to clarify how the word *phobia* is used in other cases, which have nothing to do with the present controversy. Let us take, as an example, another kind of phobia, which differs (in its spelling) by only one letter, but is a million miles away from our subject; *hemophobia*.

In an enlightening article about the latter,[65] Professor Tanya Byron says the following:

> "A phobia is developed in response to a situation that elicits significant anxiety. Being phobic literally means avoidance at all costs as the brain perceives a threat and acute anxiety is triggered. This results in immediate physiological, psycho-logical and behavioural changes that lead to fight, flight or freeze – a primitive in-built survival mechanism.
>
> Hemophobia is the extreme and irrational fear of blood, a condition in which a person is likely to faint at the sight of blood, physical injury, or the anticipation of an injection, which is why it is called blood-injury-needle phobia, because those are the panic triggering cues."

She then goes on to describe recommended treatment for the condition. Her description of what constitutes a phobia is

---

[65] "Column on Family Problems," *The Times Newspaper* (3 November, 2014), London.

the standard understanding. The question we need to ask, in the context of exploring the misuse of homophobia, is whether this understanding of phobia could possibly fit those who object to homosexual practices.

On the website of the charity, Mind, a phobia is described as:

> "an extreme form of fear or anxiety triggered by a particular situation or object, even when there is no danger. A fear becomes a phobia if it...has significant impact on how daily life is negotiated."[66]

The article goes on to describe some of the symptoms associated with phobias: feeling out of touch with reality or detached from one's body; fear of fainting; fear of losing control, fear of dying. If the symptoms are very intense, they could trigger a panic attack.

When it comes to homophobia, the way the word is currently used does not fit the clinical understanding of phobia at all. It is also included in lists that describe negative attitudes towards certain categories of people, terms that denote particular anti-ethnic, anti-demographic or anti-religious sentiments, such as Francophobia, Xenophobia, Islamophobia. The term phobia is used as an analogy to the much more precise definition used in psychiatric medical terminology. The broader use includes not only fear (its proper etymological derivation), but dislike, disapproval, prejudice, hatred, discrimination, antipathy, contempt, aversion and hostility. In other words, *phobia* is being attached to *homo* in an abnormal and idiosyncratic sense. In the interests of a careful and concise use of language, it ought not to exist. If someone is accused of being homophobic, they have a right to reply, "what makes you think that I have an extreme and irrational fear of same (homo) – sex relations?"

---

[66] Accessed 6th November, 2014.

The pro-homosexual campaigning group, Stonewall, describes homophobia as:

> "the irrational hatred, intolerance and fear of lesbian, homosexual and bi-sexual people. . .These negative feelings fuel the myths, stereotypes and discrimination that can lead to violence against LGB people."

This definition has the advantage of being a little more focused, although the meaning of some of the words used, such as *irrational*, *myths*, and *discrimination* are, themselves, in need of careful pinning down. At least, the extremely sweeping use of *prejudice* does not occur. That a person is prejudiced about some belief or action is basically in the eye of the beholder. It has now come to mean predominantly holding beliefs with which I disagree. In a literal sense, everyone is prejudiced, in that they form their current opinions on the basis of convictions (judgements) that they already hold and bring with them (hence the suffix, pre) to their understanding of the issue.

Another word often used in connection with the condemnation of homosexual practices is *bigoted*. However, the word refers only to someone who is intolerant of another's opinion or behaviour *without any just cause*. It may be applied, for example, to someone who is plainly ignorant of or deliberately misrepresents the opinion of another, or who refuses to recognise the overwhelming arguments in favour of a belief. It cannot be applied (although it often is) to anyone who simply disagrees, on good rational grounds, with the opinion of another. In the case of the debate about homosexuality, to call others bigoted is simply to vilify them. It is used as a recourse to defame a person's character; it is an *ad hominem* piece of abuse that obviates taking their point of view seriously.

So, is there a genuinely correct way of using homophobia (or preferably a much more precise term), one that takes seriously its etymological origin, and refuses to do what homosexual activists accuse their opponents of doing; namely using it to stereotype others? Unfortunately, some people, averse to homosexual relationships, have chosen to personalise their condemnation by denigrating, universally, the character of people who openly declare themselves to be lesbian or gay. This may lead to holding them in contempt, treating them as though they were lesser humans, or even less than normal humans. Such attitudes have led to the accusation, with some merit, of stigmatisation, bullying, hate-speech and even violence against homosexual people. Where the personal reputation of individuals is maligned by these kinds of attitudes and actions, they can genuinely be classified as thoroughly obnoxious and dangerously threatening, *for opposition to the practice has spilled over into animosity against the person*. This is an inexcusable misunderstanding about how civilised debate should be carried out.

It is possible that, in some cases, irrational fear of homosexuals is the motivating force that produces acts of aggression. It is also possible that the fear is the result of acute anxiety in the face of unusual and abnormal desires and practices. It has been suggested, for example, that excessively hostile reactions arise from fear that the extension of rights to homosexual couples marks the beginning of the end of the family as a unit, comprising a father, mother and their offspring. Much less plausibly, gay activists sometimes imply that homophobia is a manifestation of repressed sexual desires for one's own sex. In most cases, such an insinuation is absurd and demeans those who make it. Also, improbably, homophobia has been attributed to the concern parents may feel towards the influence that gay activists could have over the emerging sexual identity of their adolescent children.

Anxiety can be caused by the assumption that, where a society not only condones homosexual relations, but also promotes them as a perfectly healthy alternative sexual activity, this is a supreme example of moral confusion and indifference, in which boundaries between right and wrong have been obliterated. So, homosexuality is perceived as a distressing illustration of the moral bankruptcy of contemporary secular societies in the Western world. When anxiety leads to irrational fear and fear is externalised in acts of personal abuse and physical assault, it may rightly be called homophobia.

However, when some gay activists accuse the perpetrators of homophobia of extreme acts of ill-treatment towards homosexuals and of suffering themselves from a severe mental disorder, their reasoning has descended to the level of those they condemn. They are just as guilty, as are their critics, of overreacting by personalising their intense loathing of their detractors. These responses, on both sides of the controversy, do nothing to advance understanding and an honest, open and principled moral debate, that might lead to a greater discernment of the real issues. When the terms homophobia and homophobic are applied to genuine disapproval of homosexual behaviour, based either on principled and well-founded moral objections, on the accumulated evidence of its detrimental effects or on the physical and mental suffering of those who *wish to change* but are denied carefully approved counselling, there is little chance that a rational, civilised exchange of views will take place. All we are left with, sadly, is a struggle for power: a contest to see who may win the battle to impose their beliefs on the rest of society, irrespective of a proper engagement with the matters in dispute. In order to substantiate the way in which I believe the word homophobia may, and may not, be correctly used, I will turn to these objections.

The causes of same-sex attraction

Gay activists would dearly like to cut the Gordian knot of the whole controversy about homosexual relations by being able to assert, with indisputable evidence, that homosexual orientation[67] is inherited in the same kind of way as height, skin, eye and hair colour, left or right-handedness, aptitude for languages or musical ability. If it really was simply and wholly a matter of nature, the kind of person one was born to be, there would be little to discuss.

It is not surprising, therefore, that promoters of homosexuality declare that it is a wholly natural and normal state of affairs. It is argued that the inborn nature of orientation to the same sex is manifested in early childhood, particularly by boys who prefer the company of girls and enjoy participating in their activities more than those of their own sex. The development of their sexuality simply takes a different path from that of most boys. Thus, it is not to be counted as an abnormality, even less as an illness. It is the result of genetic, hormonal or brain influences over which they have no control. As a result, homosexual disposition should be considered quite usual, although not common; some people are just born gay. The heterosexual community, therefore, should become accustomed to accepting the fact.

Following on from this premise, gay activists have persuaded much of Western society to include homosexuality among a list of protected groups, alongside race, ethnicity, gender, disability and age. Likewise, homophobia is aligned to racism, sexism, anti-Semitism and ageism. Now, if homosexuality were wholly determined by pre-birth factors in such a

---

[67] So controversial and contested is language in the arena of homosexual discourse that the word orientation should also be questioned. The word suggests that homosexuality is a fixed, inherited state, that is permanent and immovable. If one were to use other words, such as inclination, disposition, tendency, preference or attraction, they would undoubtedly convey a different nuance. There is, unfortunately, no neutral terminology that all sides in the debate would find satisfactory. As I believe that there is overwhelming evidence to indicate that homosexual awareness is not either a wholly inherited trait nor set for all time, I will avoid the term. In other words, for the sake of clarity and integrity, I will use other terms, which I believe more adequately express and explain the reality of homosexual relationships.

way that it could be compared to race or gender, there would not be much cause for argument. Considerations of equality and anti-discrimination should be applied with the same criteria and force. Homosexuals, then, if they do not receive identical treatment to that accorded to women, and people of all races and ages, could rightly claim the status of victims of illogical prejudice. Nobody has chosen their gender, their ethnic background or the day on which they were born. Nobody, by the same token, has chosen their sexuality. The human race is simply split into two parts: those attracted to the opposite sex (the majority) and those attracted to their own sex (the minority). This is the reality of people's biological make-up.

Now, if this were the case, and although some genetically-influenced traits are generally considered undesirable (the disposition to be obese or prone to alcoholism being obvious examples), homosexuality would hardly be a major issue. However, there are good reasons for concluding that homosexuality, although minimally influenced by pre-birth factors, is largely the result of what psychiatrists call environmental circumstances and personal choices.

Nature more than nurture?

For approximately 70 years, from the beginning of the 20th century, psychiatric practice considered homosexual inclination and behaviour to be a neurosis. As the result of a solid body of research, built up over these years, the main cause was located in dysfunctional relationships between a male child and his father and a female child and her mother. The result of these impaired relationships, according to the theory, was that neither sex was able to come to terms with its own gender identity.

As the process of sexual imprinting begins in early childhood, and given the importance to that process of a healthy bonding with the same gender parent, when it does not happen, the child is likely to suffer from a crisis of gender identity. Karl Jung, referring to his clinical work with homosexuals, believed that, because a man has failed to find maleness deep within his inner being, he attempts to find it at the biological-sexual level. Anna Freud located the motivational factor for homosexual desire in the search by the male to "repair" his identification with the male gender, which he failed to achieve as a boy.

The factors in the relationship which have not worked for the boy may be the father's perceived absence from the home, or the lack of a father altogether, or an overbearing father who communicates harsh judgements and severe punishments to the child; rarely if ever balanced by warm affection and compassionate care. As a result, the child turns to the mother for consolation and protection and, as the years go by, is never able to break free from the mother's well-meant, but nevertheless stifling, embrace. The failure of the male child to discover his masculinity, would be due to the fact that his only close role model about male identity has been an alienated and alienating figure.

Homosexual disposition is interpreted, therefore, as the attempt by the adolescent or young adult to compensate for the failure to find a proper male role model in early childhood by later seeking someone of his own sex with whom to identify. If the theory is correct, at least in a number of cases of homosexual attraction, it might help to account for the fact that homosexual behaviour is often promiscuous. The elusive ideal male can never be found.[68]

The consensus of clinicians involved in attending to people with a homosexual disposition led, by the early 1960s, to a considered judgement by the New York Academy of Medicine that "homosexuality is indeed an illness. The homosexual is an emotionally disturbed individual who has not acquired normal

---

[68] There are also other reasons, which we will discuss further on, why many homosexuals appear to enjoy numerous sexual partners.

capacity to develop satisfying heterosexual relations."[69] Ten years later, the American Psychiatric Association removed homosexuality from its list of disorders.[70] The rest, as they say, is history.

Although huge pressure has been, and continues to be, put on psychiatric practice not to continue to investigate the likely causes of homosexual attraction, research does continue to take place. Besides the apparently harmful consequences of dysfunctional parenting, it has been noted that a much higher percentage of homosexuals than occurs in the heterosexual community have reported sexual abuse in childhood by same-sex adults. Of course, the correlation of data of this nature does not amount to proof of cause. However, when the statistics are repeated in a number of independent and controlled surveys, the coincidences do suggest some kind of causal link.

Gradually, a consensus is building amongst psychiatric practitioners that homosexual attraction is influenced by a number of different factors. It is fairly certain that it does not originate in the DNA code. Studies of identical twins, who inherit the same genetic variables, demonstrate that where one declares himself or herself to be gay or lesbian, on average,

---

[69] Naturally, the LGBT community strongly rejects this judgement, for reasons that will become apparent in the course of our survey.

[70] There is no space to outline the processes by which this sudden, complete reversal of conventional psychiatric understanding of the homosexual condition took place. Suffice it to say, most commentators, including those supportive of same-sex behaviour, describe the main cause for the change to be intense political campaigning by the pro-homosexual lobby. Bayer, Ronald in his book, *Homosexuality and American Psychiatry: The Politics of Diagnosis,* (1987), Princeton, Princeton University Press, states that the decision was not based on the appropriation of scientific evidence based on research, but on action demanded by the ideological temper of the times. The main issue was political, namely the question of who decides what is normal sexuality. Seeing that, according to the protagonists of change, this cannot be decided scientifically, it has to be resolved in the arena of public opinion. The decision-makers in the APA were persuaded that homosexual behaviour is simply a perfectly natural, well-adjusted alternative to heterosexual relations.

around 11% of the other twins do the same. Although this is a much higher average than the approximately 3% of self-declared LGBT people in society as a whole, for the source of homosexuality to be exclusively genetically-based, it would need to be 100%. Moreover, cross-cultural studies have confirmed that homosexual attraction varies considerably across different societies.[71] As the human race shares between 99.7 and 99.9% of genes, one would expect same-sex attraction to be similar in all cultures, if it is wholly due to genetic factors. The data, however, shows a wide diversity.

Likewise, inherent differences in brain structure or brain functioning between homosexuals and heterosexuals have not been found. No replicable scientific study has yet shown any differences between the brains of adult homosexuals and heterosexuals. It has been shown, however, that brains are extraordinarily plastic, in the sense that the way they function is influenced considerably by the circumstances through which a person lives and by the choices they make. Repeated thought and behaviour alter the brain's micro-structure, and these changes can be picked up by brain scans. In the case of alcoholics, for example, there may be a propensity towards addiction that is built into either one's genetic endowment or brain structure, or even hormonal activity related to a mother's lifestyle. Nevertheless, none of these elements determines that one will inevitably become an alcoholic in later life. The fact is that neither our genes nor our environment compel us to do anything; in the last analysis, behaviour is a matter of choice. Whatever the influences and circumstances, we are free to say yes or no to certain courses of action.

---

[71] Duggan, Lisa in her 'Afterword' to Katz, *The Invention of Heterosexuality*, (2007), 2nd edition, p. 195, denies the 'essentialist' argument that lesbians, gay men and bisexuals are born, not made. Her argument is based on the conviction that both homosexuality and heterosexuality are historical social conventions, not naturally and eternally given: "Sexual identity", she says, "is cross-culturally and historically variable."

Responses to the causes of same-sex attraction

Within the LGBT community, there have been a number of different responses to the research findings summarised above. Some maintain, dogmatically, that same-sex attraction is innate in a person's biological make-up. Richard Isay, for example, states quite categorically that genetic factors, along with the balance of hormones in the womb, are shown to be decisive in the origin of sexual orientation.[72] Therefore, he concludes that homosexual love and passion are not bad, sinful or sick. However, he does admit that a considerable body of analysts still believe that heterosexuality is the only normal outcome of psycho-sexual development.

Others are convinced by the accumulated evidence that there are a number of different circumstances involved in causing a small minority of people, at least in Western societies, to turn to homosexual practices. Genetic constitutions probably play a part, but so do the circumstantial aspects of parenting, education, early sexual-abuse and peer influences. Nevertheless, whatever the factors involved, some people find themselves erotically drawn towards their own sex and unable to relate intimately to the opposite sex.

They conclude, therefore, that such people should be allowed, indeed encouraged, to act out their sexual impulses without fear of condemnation. This is simply the way they are. They would argue that the expectation that normal sexual tendency is towards the other sex, and that therefore homosexuality is abnormal, is simply a social construction, based on prejudice. If these people wish to engage in exclusive same-sex relationships, society should not presume to condemn them or try to intervene; they should be free from social and

---

[72] *Being Homosexual: Gay Men and their Development,* (2009), p. xvi, New York, Vintage Books. He quotes the studies assembled in Wilson, Glenn and Rahman, Qazi *Born Gay: The Psychobiology of Sex Orientation,* (2005), London, Peter Owen Publishers.

legal sanctions, pressurising them to conform to the arbitrary norm of heterosexuality.[73]

Yet others have embraced a much more libertarian attitude to homosexual relationships. Beginning from the observation that, as only a small percentage of the population identify themselves as gay or lesbian, the survival of the human species is not at risk from the inability of same-sex couples to produce the next generation. They argue that, for some, pleasure in sexual performance has displaced the objective of procreation. It is an end in itself, to be enjoyed purely for its own sake. Some have even gone as far as to assert that in an age of consumption, renunciation, restraint and inhibition are to be perceived as outmoded and discredited virtues. Sexual encounters, when reciprocal and consensual, whether heterosexual or homosexual, are to be taken advantage of, as if they were legitimate possessions. It is hypocritical of 'straight' people to condemn the often-multiple liaisons of gay men and (to a lesser extent) lesbians, when they themselves may well use the services of prostitutes or other willing participants of the other sex for 'one-night-stands.'

Change of 'orientation'?

The homosexual community is not known for its ability to agree on a number of the issues that have so far been raised. However, on one matter, most are adamant. It is not legitimate for anyone to attempt to help gay or lesbian people change their disposition from homosexual to heterosexual. Twenty years after the landmark decision of the APA to remove homosexuality from the list of disorders, it considered altering its code of ethics to make it a violation of professional conduct for a psychiatrist to help a homosexual patient become heterosexual, even at the patient's request. Such practices, through

---

[73] See Katz, Jonathan Ned (2007/2), *The Invention of Heterosexuality*, Chicago, University of Chicago Press.

inducing guilt and shame, were likened, using extravagant and exaggerated language, to brainwashing and conversion techniques.

Recently published professional guidelines in the United Kingdom affirm that it is an ethical offence either to offer to help a client to overcome homosexual temptations and feelings or to accede to a request to do so. The reasoning behind this is two-fold: first, to offer treatment that might 'cure' or 'reduce' same-sex attraction is "to offer treatment for which there is no illness;" secondly, the client's request for therapy for reduction of same-sex attraction is not in the client's best interests, on the assumption that such therapy produces greater trauma and confusion than that, presumably, already being experienced by the client making the request.[74] This stance, however, is quite perverse for numerous reasons. Firstly, most medical ethics' directions in the Western world have adopted, as a fundamental guiding principle, the autonomy and self-expressed concerns of the patient. In the case of homosexual attraction, however, their concerns apparently should not be admitted. The only kind of therapy permitted is that which assists the evidently disorientated client to accept and live out, free from inhibitions, his sexual 'orientation'.

Secondly, the stance is hypocritical, in that gay activists encourage people who believe they are predisposed to same-sex affections to 'come out' and declare to the world that they are indeed homosexually disposed, yet they react with anger if anyone dares to claim that they are ex-gay. This seems to suggest that society welcomes and encourages diversity and inclusivity, except in the case of anyone wishing to leave a same-sex lifestyle and of therapists who agree to help them achieve their desire.

---

[74] See the 'Consensus Statement' (June 2014) of a group of professional psychiatric and psychotherapeutic bodies, www.psychotherapy.org.uk/consensus ; also the Royal College of Psychiatrists, 'Statement on Sexual Orientation (PS02)', April 2014, www. rcpsych.ac.uk.

Thirdly, it is now not uncommon for respected institutions, like the World Health Organisation and the British Royal College of Psychiatrists, to state that homosexuals can change. The latter has said, "it is not the case that sexual orientation is immutable or might not vary to some extent in a person's life."[75] Indeed, it is increasingly being recognised by serious research that sexual inclinations are not rigid, but pliant along a scale ranging from apparently enduring same-sex sentiments through various degrees of bi-sexuality to permanent other-sex attraction. There is overwhelming evidence that, particularly in adolescence, young people who identify as gay or lesbian one year are likely to label themselves as heterosexual the next.

Fourthly, no convincing, reproducible evidence has been attested to confirm that change therapy is always and everywhere harmful, or that it can never be advantageous. In a celebrated case in the UK, a homosexual journalist, under false pretences, sought counselling to change his sexual 'orientation'. When the therapist in question, in totally good faith, assuming that the client was genuine, agreed to offer help, she was denounced as someone who exploited people's unfounded anxieties about their sexuality. Her professional accrediting body removed her licence to practise. However, at an appeal hearing against the loss of her livelihood, the person who had enlisted her professional support said he was not seeking to challenge the efficiency of reorientation therapy, since he had no evidence to say that such therapy was not beneficial for some clients. This was an appalling case of deceit and doublethink.

Fifthly, forbidding the possibility of seeking counselling for a change towards heterosexuality completely ignores the considerable number of personal testimonies of people who claim that, in their case, such clinical assistance has achieved the end they sought. Homosexual activists are driven

---

[75] 'Statement on Sexual Orientation.'

to make the absurd claim that such people are demonstrating pathological symptoms, from which they need to be delivered. Homosexuality, they argue, cannot be counted as an illness, but the request to be free from homosexual desires is a disorder (called 'internalised homophobia' – the homosexual's negative image of themselves that is alleged to come from the shame and guilt associated with not conforming to the cultural expectation that heterosexuality is what men and women should desire). To stoop to the tactic of declaring people, who confirm themselves to be ex-gay, dishonest is, itself, a dishonest strategy made by the people who make the accusation and degrading to those who are so accused. How could such an attitude possibly be counted as respecting another person's conviction? It smacks of professional authoritarianism and unjustifiable intolerance.

The reasons we have put forward for condemning the attitude that denies the right of homosexuals to seek help to change their orientation, if they freely and sincerely wish to avail themselves of such counselling, suggest that another agenda is at work here. The standard response of professional associations has been that there is considerable emotional and psychological cost associated with change therapies, and that the main impulse that drives people to seek help to change is internalised homophobia.[76]

In the case of those seeking psychiatric help for emotional distress and confusion (*of whatever kind*), one would assume that they will not be expecting to encounter an easy-going, superficial and merely pacifying treatment of their deeply felt anguish and pain. The therapist may well take them through, as gently and sensitively as possible, traumatic experiences of

---

[76] The 'Consensus Statement' cites evidence selectively that only supports their case. It ignores counter-evidence; for example, that of Jones & Yarhouse, (2011), which shows modest success can be achieved, and did not find any harm resulting from the therapy; see, the discussion of Ould, Peter, http://www.peter-ould.net/2011/09/30/jones-and-yarhouses-exgay-study/

the past, in order to bring healing to upsetting memories that have been suppressed, because of the anguish they would otherwise bring. There can be no guarantee that the outcome of counselling will be exactly according to the client's wishes. However, in many cases, it has been shown to achieve, without any long-term negative effects, the change being sought.

The problem for the gay lobby is that, if counselling leads to a successful 'orientation' change or modification, the notion that sexual predisposition is constitutional and immutable is disproven. That, surely, is the real reason for disallowing reparative therapy. If former self-identifying homosexuals are able to build normal, healthy, heterosexual relationships, because that is what they wish to do, then the belief that homosexual 'orientation' is unavoidably permanent and unchangeable is left without any substantial support. It is not surprising, then, that a pro-homosexual clinician like Richard Isay would say that it is helpful, clinically, to start from the presupposition that gay and lesbian identity is innate, and to work with clients to reinforce the acceptance of and delight in their sexual propensity. However, the cost of making this a priori judgement is to deny the client the right to change his or her self-identity.

In the case of internalised homophobia, the evidence is ambiguous. The fear of being identified as gay or lesbian may be correlated with an insecurity about masculine or feminine identity that leads to denial or repression. Some see this as the main reason why so few sports people self-identify as homosexual. However, such cases are a long way from demonstrating that all requests for help to mitigate or change homosexual feelings have the same common element. The familiar assertion that therapy for change is futile and damages self-esteem is simply false. One has to conclude, therefore, that the common claim that such therapy is harmful is only true in an ideological, not empirical, sense: it harms the standard pro-homosexual article of faith that the orientation is inborn and unchangeable.

There are a number of perfectly rational reasons why people might want to seek help to increase their heterosexual potential. In some cases, it will issue from a clash of moral values. The person concerned is persuaded that homosexual practices are considered wrong by the belief system to which they adhere. When faced with the choice of celibacy or the possibility of significant re-orientation, they choose to explore the latter. Perhaps, the most common reason would be the desire to experience normal family life with the possibility of bearing one's own children. A further reason might be to leave a lifestyle that has been shown to be much more open to the substantial risk of sexually transmitted infections than that of the heterosexual community. Another example might be that of a married man with children, who feels himself being torn away from his family by his unwanted same-sex attraction.

There are at least three fundamental ethical considerations to be taken into account when agreeing to provide therapeutic counselling for those desiring a change of orientation. Firstly, the counsellor must respect the client's autonomy, i.e. their right to make an informed choice about their sexuality. This means that there should be no doctrinaire pre-judgement about the way in which an individual's sexual identity has developed or the various influences that shaped it. Secondly, there should be properly-established consent, i.e. the counsellor must be persuaded that the client has come to his or her decision on the basis of principled motives and understands the clinical procedures, the possible outcomes and the degree of stress they are likely to experience as a result of the therapy. Before counselling begins, the client should be given time to reflect on whether this is the course of action they really wish to take.[77] Thirdly, the counsellor must ascertain that there has been no external pressure from family, friends, peer groups or religious communities to seek change therapy. Counsellors must also

---

[77] Such consent, of course, would be applicable before entering therapy for any perceived adversity.

examine their own motives to make sure that they are not unduly pressing a person into making a decision that may not be in his or her best interest.

The present situation in which some counsellors are coerced into having to refuse therapies that may lead to a change in sexual attraction, because of the fear of losing their livelihood, is wholly unsatisfactory. The prohibition on such counselling is based on selective evidence, does not take into consideration alternative research findings and unwarrantably discriminates against the declared wishes of adult men and women. It cannot be said to have been arrived at with the best interests of the client in mind; rather, it would appear that it is designed to uphold a particular ideological stance that refuses to tolerate any contrary opinion on the subject of sexual identity.

The moral debate

For some in the gay rights movement, homosexual behaviour is almost beyond critical moral judgement. As long as sexual arrangements are within the law (e.g. not carried out with children or under-age adolescents), are entirely consensual (i.e. all possible forms of coercion are absent) and are carried out with due precaution against the risk of sexually-transmitted diseases, no outside agent should become involved in what is an entirely private matter. In the 21st century, the strict rules and regulations, taboos and restraints have been swept away. Neither religion, which has sought to supervise and guard sexual mores, nor the state, which hitherto, supposedly at the bidding of clergy and imams, has implemented strict controls over family life and interpersonal relations, has any legitimate role in restricting sexual activity. Public morality is not involved; what a person does with another person in private is not a matter for ethical discussion nor for the involvement of the law.

This way of thinking has come to dominate public and private discourse in the secular West. Nothing is out of bounds, as long as care is taken not to harm the interests of others. Why, then, should others disapprove of homosexual practice, seeing that it is the pursuit of a small minority of the population, who, it is claimed, do not wish to interfere with the sexual activities of the majority? These are concerns of individuals, acting out of their own understanding of what is seemly and admissible.

Moreover, science has, it is alleged, officially pronounced that homosexual 'orientation' and activity is not a disorder, but a different order. It is not an illness, because the definition of an illness is a physical or mental condition that is undesirable to the sufferer. When the APA removed homosexual inclination from its list of disorders, it simply shifted it from undesirable to desirable. If homosexuality is not an illness, there is nothing wrong with it (psychologically). If it cannot be changed, it cannot be a problem. It just is.

Why, therefore, one might ask, is there so much controversy? The answer is that people on either side of the debate are reasoning from entirely different moral frameworks. Of course, there are genuine disputes about the scientific evidence for the reality and consequences of homosexuality, but these, it is asserted, are difficult to resolve, and in any case, science, as such, provides no basis for moral decision-making. The nature of right and wrong has to be resolved on another foundation, according to one's view of the nature and purpose of human existence.

What does it mean to be human? There are only two possible answers to this question: either human beings have been designed and shaped by a supreme Being who has created them in such a way that they can only flourish when they live according to the moral directions that this Being has made available, or they are the result of a blind, evolutionary process taking place over many millions of years, that is random, and in itself purposeless (with the possible exception of survival). In the latter case, there are no instructions from elsewhere as to how we should live. We take stock of our experience and decide, on this basis, the best way to live. By and large, the homosexual community lives by the second option: what society can be persuaded not to forbid is permissible; in other words, right and wrong beliefs and actions are decided by the majority, or by those with most influence within the decision-making structures of the state. Those who are opposed to homosexual practice as a deviation from the norm of monogamous, heterosexual relationships, in the main, live by the first option: they are persuaded that knowledge of right and wrong comes as information from beyond space and time, from a personal Being (like ourselves) who has existed from eternity, brought the universe into existence and continues to act within it.

These are two intrinsically opposed versions of the grounds for moral virtues and vices, of rights and responsibilities.[78] The second version has become the default position of secular cultures, on the basis that there is no convincing evidence for the first position, which is a matter of individual conviction, based on a faith beyond reason and demonstrable proof. The concept of alleged homosexual rights has flourished in the cultural conditions made possible by the assumption that humans are autonomous, in respect of any externally-binding, absolute moral principles and codes.

Is it possible to settle this huge difference of perspective? The answer is probably no, for the simple reason that there are no universally agreed criteria for judging the correctness, or otherwise, of the basic presuppositions in each case. Science, as a methodology for discovering *how* the material world operates, is powerless to decide *how* humans should treat one

---

[78] This does not mean that there is no borrowing going on from one set of moral foundations to another. The borrowing largely happens in the case of the second option taking over the assumptions, principles and guidelines of the first option. For there to be a coherent set of moral standards, some account of absolute values must be asserted. It is well-nigh impossible to deduce these from a wholly random set of unfolding events. The second option simply cannot produce what its supporters would like to achieve.

another. There is no route from the description of what *is* to a normative moral judgement of what *ought to be*. Science can help us see the physical, psychological and emotional consequences of the moral choices we make, but cannot adjudicate between them. If, for example, a person decides that he or she will adopt an unhealthy lifestyle that will inevitably lead to premature death, medical science can only say, well, you were warned of the consequences of your preferred option; it cannot say whether such a choice was right or wrong, or even wise or foolish. If life does not have any transcendent existential purpose, the maxim, "let us eat, drink and be merry (gay?), for tomorrow we die," may be a reasonable dictum.

However, there are two caveats to the drift of this argument. Firstly, critical, methodologically-sound observation of what transpires when people choose particular courses of action does have a bearing on what is in the best interests of a society to tolerate or approve. For example, in the present discussion about the claimed rights of homosexual couples to acquire children, either through surrogacy or by adoption, the question of the optimum conditions for their nurture and well-being can be measured over time by comparing the later outcome of their lives with that of children growing up in a heterosexual family. Assuming, in both cases, a stable, caring environment and an unequivocal commitment to a monogamous relationship on the part of the parents, controlled, repeatable analyses of the effects of the different situations on the children can, and have been, discerned.

Probably, both sides of the moral debate would accept that the prerogatives of the children, who were not free to choose their family circumstances, are greater than those of the parents. Thus, if it can be shown, that homosexual couples are much more likely to separate than heterosexual ones, and that separation has a detrimental effect on the well-being of the child – both of which have been demonstrated by well-structured studies – then that is an argument against the automatic right of same-sex couples to adopt children. By the same token, if it can be shown that children develop in a more emotionally balanced way by living in a family with a father and a mother than is the case with two parents of the same gender, then it is in their interests, irrespective of the wishes of the prospective parents, not to encourage such a social experimentation.

The second caveat has to do with the way the state intervenes in the controversy surrounding homosexual relations. This takes us back to the contentious question of human rights. Do homosexuals constitute a privileged group, which has a justifiable claim to be protected against certain forms of presumed discrimination? Is there a right to form legally-recognised partnerships or marriages, with all the economic and civil privileges that are entailed? If so, from whence do these rights come? Clearly, if, as has been demonstrated, homosexuality is not comparable to race, ethnicity or gender as a reality of birth, the gay movement cannot argue for non-discrimination on the same grounds. If gay relationships are not equivalent to heterosexual ones, a fact that is simply shown by an examination of the differences, then no claims can be made on the basis of equal rights.[79]

So, when governments legislate in favour of 'gay rights,' what moral justification can they put forward? If the reality of homosexual behaviour is more a choice than a predetermined and immutable disposition, as many homosexuals admit, what are the grounds for favouring this choice? By passing laws to secure special privileges for this particular community, other groups, in order to defend consciences, will almost certainly have to defy the law at certain points. Legalising practices that, a generation or so ago, were deemed to be the result of a dysfunctional identity tends to bring the law into disrepute and unnecessary conflict into public life.

---

[79] I have shown the empirical differences between the two sets of relationship in the chapter on equality; see, pp. 56-59.

The result is a string of quite unnecessary prosecutions against people whose perfectly valid convictions do not allow them to take part in actions that compromise their beliefs. The state simply causes needless dissension by intervening on one side of a moral debate that has not been settled by force of rational argument, but by acts of arbitrary power. The unduly rapid rush to pass measures into law that favour a minority community and discriminate against a larger community is hardly the act of a discerning democracy. It is based, as we have discussed in previous chapters, on a false understanding of key ideas, such as discrimination, tolerance, equality and rights. In the concluding section of this chapter, I wish to suggest a better, ultimately more prudent and practical public policy.

Conclusions

The causes of homosexuality

This analysis of the main reasons why the grounds for using the term homophobia should, in most cases, be rejected is based on a number of assumptions. Firstly, and most crucially, that the most objective research into same-sex attraction has concluded that it is neither innate, inherited nor irreversible; there are a range of factors in a person's constitution and life circumstances that contribute to its occurrence. Secondly, because the preference is not predetermined, there is a telling element of choice in opting for homosexual relationships. Thirdly, for these reasons, homosexuality is a reality wholly different in kind from race and gender. The latter are irrefutably a matter of birth; no choice is involved. Homophobia, when put in the same category as racism and sexism, indicating in the latter cases a settled malice and hostility against people of a particular race or gender, is illegitimately used of people accused of similar attitudes towards people living a homosexual lifestyle. It simply exhibits a terminological confusion.

The nature of sexuality

Although homosexual acts have been condoned in a variety of societies over a long period of history, most notoriously, at the height of Greek and Roman civilisations, an established condition of homosexuality is an invention of the Western world, originating about 150 years ago. Before the 19th century, there is no evidence that any society recorded the existence of a gay and lesbian minority, or even discernible gay and lesbian-oriented individuals. *Being* gay is a relatively recent social construction. This reality is another reason for denying any equivalence between homosexual and heterosexual arrangements; the latter, as orders of human societies, go back as far as the dawn of human history.

Same-sex, erotic attraction and behaviour is fluid and changeable. Statistical surveys establish the reality that around 50% of those who, at one time, declare themselves to be gay or lesbian will move towards settled heterosexual conduct at a later stage of their lives. In the 16-17 years age-group, 98% will move from homosexual intimations to an established heterosexual orientation within a year or two. Homosexuality may simply be a short phase that adolescents go through, as they experiment with sudden, new emotional desires.

It is quite wrong, therefore, for anyone to suggest that, because of casual same-sex liaisons at a young age, some young people are homosexual by nature. Sexuality, in the real world, is pliant and polymorphous. Young people, in particular, are prone to experiment; they are less likely to be bothered by the risks associated with multiple partners of either sex. Unless they have strong convictions in the area of sexual morality, leading to abstinence or restraint, they are quite likely to engage in sexual acts, whenever the right occasion presents itself.[80]

---

[80] There is some recent, circumstantial evidence, however, that the millennial generation is less casual in its sexual practices than those that have immediately preceded it.

The language of homophobia

It should now be clear that in, a large number of cases where *homophobia* is used as the description of an attitude towards practising gays and lesbians, or *homophobic* as an adjective applied to individual instances of the attitude, the words are used in an inaccurate and indiscriminate manner. There is little doubt that, in many situations, it is used as a pejorative word of abuse, to foreclose an open, rational discussion of the reality of homosexuality, its place in society and its moral status. Far too often it is used as an *ad hominem* technique; simply using the term itself to discredit those who oppose certain manifestations of homosexuality.

It is incorrect to suggest that principled objections to the theory and practice of homosexuality and opposition to some of the tactics employed by gay activists to secure social and legal recognition for their state amount to the violation of a person's dignity and worth. Even less do they amount to the desire to create a hostile, humiliating or offensive environment. The extravagant use of the terminology is a not-so-subtle attempt to force an entire population to embrace an alien moral framework. Its effect may well be counter-productive, increasing negative sentiments towards homosexuals.

So, are there situations where the language of homophobia (or less inaccurate synonyms) may be used properly? I would suggest that, in accordance with the etymology of the word phobia, the use of the term homophobia should be limited to manifestations of *irrational* fear of either homosexual behaviour or the destructive influence of pro-homosexual campaigning on the moral fabric of society, or both. By irrational, in this context, one means attitudes and beliefs that are based on wild speculations about the impact of homosexuality on social structures, leading to conspiracy theories, misrepresentations, generalisations and scape-goating. For example, some people are inclined to believe that all, or a majority of, practising homosexuals are predators who molest children, seduce young people, flaunt their sexuality, proselytise for homosexual lifestyles, encourage promiscuity, spread disease and advocate the destruction of the family.[81] The problem with this view is not that individuals, or a few groups, who do some or all of these things, cannot be found, but that a large company of people are tarred with the same brush. It is the blanket condemnation of people who prefer a certain course of behaviour, as if they all were prone to the worst possible motives and actions.

As we discussed earlier, fear becomes a phobia when it results in acute anxiety that becomes an obsession and consumes a person's life. Then, it is likely to lead to intense dislike, physical aversion and loathing. When it becomes a nagging compulsion, it will probably end up in justifying acts of hatred towards known people, including extreme verbal abuse (such as bullying), ostracism and physical violence.

Homophobia should only be reserved for these types of expression of hostility and malice towards individuals or groups. It should not be used as a catch-all phrase aimed at all people who believe, on well-considered moral and practical grounds, that homosexual activity is unnatural, abnormal and aberrant. We have striven to show that objections to homosexuality are based on both principled ethical criteria and good, solid scientific research. These objections are particularly directed at gay and lesbian activists who continually mislead the public about the real nature and effects of homosexual lifestyles, and who lobby intensely to gain special rights and privileges for their community.

Ways ahead?

Nothing that has been said in this chapter, though robust in the present sexually permissive climate, could fairly be

---

[81] See, Fone, Byrne *Homophobia: A History,* (2001), New York, Picador.

construed as homophobic, as long as the word is used in a careful, non-emotional way. However, as the terminology is bandied about in a cavalier fashion, I have no doubt that, even though I have attempted to discuss in a serious and sober manner, some of the main issues to do with the homosexual agenda and the rapidity with which supposed homosexual rights have been granted in most parts of the Western world, that is how I will be branded. If that is the case, it will be further evidence for my thesis that the language of homophobia is being abused and used largely as a term of abuse.

What is needed in the highly-charged debate about the reality of homosexuality in contemporary, secular and religious moral discourse is a sense of perspective. Since the Wolfenden Report, published in 1957 on behalf of the British Home Office,[82] numerous pieces of legislation have been passed to alter the legal status of practising homosexuals. The first act was to decriminalise consenting adult homosexual relationships. This was based on the supposition that there is "a realm of private morality and immorality which is, in brief and crude terms, not the law's business."[83] This was not intended to be an endorsement of the activity, but, as in the case of adultery, not to confuse what some would consider to be a sinful act with a criminal offence. Although, at the time (the late 1960s), no attempt was made to repeal laws that made sodomy and other acts of 'gross indecency' indictable, these were no longer pursued by law-enforcement agencies.

The next major step in recognising legal rights for gay and lesbian partnerships came in the *Civil Partnership Act* in England and Wales in 2004. This allowed same-sex couples to obtain, essentially, the same rights and responsibilities as married opposite-sex couples: property rights, social security and pension benefits, the same exemptions on inheritance tax,

---

[82] *Report of the Committee on Homosexual Offences and Prostitution,* (1957), chaired by Lord Wolfenden, London, Home Office.
[83] *Report of the Committee. . .*

the ability to exercise parental responsibility for a partner's child, the same claims for reasonable maintenance of one's partner (and child), tenancy rights, full life-insurance recognition and next-of-kin rights. There is also a formal process for dissolving partnerships, akin to divorce. In 2013, in England and Wales (and, before that, in many other Western nations and some US States) *The Marriage (Same-Sex Couples) Act* legalised same-sex marriage, starting in March 2014, whilst allowing civil partnerships to remain available. The reason for taking this last unprecedented step was spelt out, rather crudely, by David Cameron, the then British Prime Minister:

> "I am proud that we have made same-sex marriage happen. I am delighted that the love two people have for each other – and the commitment they want to make – can now be recognised as equal. I have backed this reform because I believe in commitment, responsibility and family. I don't want to see people's love divided by law. Making marriage available to everyone says so much about the society that we are and the society that we want to live in – one which respects individuals regardless of their sexuality. If a group is told again and again that they are less valuable, over time they may start to believe it. In addition to the personal damage that this can cause, it inhibits the potential of a nation. For this reason too, I am pleased that we have had the courage to change."[84]

What is fascinating about the debate leading up to the passing of these two Acts is how much of the changes that have come about are due to the mishandling of precisely some of the language I have analysed in this whole study. I have already indicated that, for example, the concept of 'equal marriage' is a complete misnomer, since there is no equivalence

---

[84] Quoted in the *London Evening Standard*, 18th July, 2013.

between same-sex and opposite-sex marriage. Homosexual relationships, however permanent they are intended to be, simply do not fulfil the conditions to be recognised as marriage. Anyone can marry in the proper sense, as long as they don't contravene the conditions for marriage, by being already married, being below the minimum legal age, wishing to marry close blood relatives or wanting to have more than one married partner. People with a same-sex attraction can also marry, as long as they fulfil the condition of finding someone of the opposite sex to marry. There is, therefore, no more discrimination against disallowing homosexual people to marry than against a child of 14, a man taking a second wife or a widower wishing to marry his daughter. Surely, the coining of the term 'equal-marriage' was a brilliant linguistic coup in the spirit of Jonathan Katz's quote at the beginning of this chapter:

> "...Human beings use words to create particular perceptions of the world, on which they then act, and alter the social institutions around them."

Exactly so! Though, as a champion of alleged homosexual rights, he may have meant his comment in a different sense!

Likewise, it is disingenuous to complain of having a right to marry taken away, when there was never a right in the first place. In a recent judgement, the European Court of Human Rights made clear that there is no such phenomenon as a right to marry, for people of the same gender. A claim to a right cannot be summoned at will. Such capricious claims are an abuse of the whole notion of human rights as the protection of legitimate freedoms against arbitrary interference by the state. Love simply does not come into it.

No doubt there are many cases, when a man of 18 will claim to love a girl of 14, a man with one wife will claim to have fallen in love with another woman and exert his right to marry her, without divorcing the first one, and a father will claim to love his daughter in an erotic relationship. To allege the overriding emotion of love (whatever this may mean as a catch-all justification) does not entitle people to campaign for a certain status for which they do not qualify. Cameron shows a profound lack of judgement, if he thinks that legislating for same-sex marriage will strengthen family life. He lacks insight, if he believes that the denial of something that does not exist lessens a person's value as a human being. Human value is based on something far more fundamental than the ideological act of consenting to a particular group's political offensive.

No doubt there are people of the same sex who have formed a profound friendship, which they have not been able to make with a person of the opposite sex, wish to live together, and their living together may include sexual acts, done in private. It is not the business of the state to interfere in such a relationship: either to make it unlawful or to give it some special credence by giving it specific legal recognition. As a matter of fact, this is precisely all that many gay and lesbian people wish for: to recognise the acceptability of such a relationship, free from stigma, harassment, the threat of blackmail or any other kind of intimidation. Same sex affinity and affection can be a beautiful relationship, without having to be elevated into some kind of special standing within the law. The writer Richard Waghorne, himself a self-declared homosexual, puts the whole matter into perspective when he says:

"Explaining that you oppose gay marriage as a gay man tends to get a baffled response at first. This is understandable given *how quickly the debate on gay marriage can collapse into allegations of homophobia.*..I have watched with growing irritation as principled opponents of gay marriage have put up with a stream of abuse for explaining their position. Public figures who have tried to do so routinely have to contend with the charge that they are bigoted or homophobic...The reflex response from many gay marriage advocates is to paint all dissent as prejudice, as if the only reason for defending marriage as it has existed to date is some variety of bigotry or psychological imbalance...Surely it is time to have a proper conversation about gay marriage...Only then will the essence and real reason for supporting traditional marriage be allowed to come to the fore again. The best interests of the children of the nation must always come first."[85]

This statement is certainly part of what I mean by perspective. The whole debate about homosexuality is out of all proportion to its significance within the life of a society. The abusive use of the term homophobia caricatures and exacerbates the discussion. Therefore, I would suggest another word be found to refer to those who oppose homosexual relationships, not on the grounds of blind ignorance or irrational fanaticism, but on carefully considered and well thought-through moral criteria; otherwise, the debate will continue to descend into mindless mud-slinging, vacuous insults and gratuitous defamation. The word homonegativity/ homonegative has been suggested as an alternative. As the opposite of negative would be constructive, the term does not appeal as a productive preference. Other possible choices might be homo-dissent or homo-disapproval; but these do not exactly trip off the tongue. My preferred suggestion would be homocritique/homocritical. These words, whilst clearly implying opposition to pro-homosexual behaviour and propaganda, also convey an intelligent, thoughtful and well-balanced survey of all the contentious issues that surround homosexuality. At least, they would have the merit of being used in their proper sense.

---

[85] 'Gay marriage', *The Irish Daily Mail*, April 5th, 2011 (emphasis added).

Select bibliography

Bayer, Ronald, (1987), *Homosexuality and American Psychiatry: The Politics of Diagnosis*, Princeton, Princeton University Press

Dumphy, Richard, (2000), *Sexual Politics: An Introduction*, (Edinburgh, Edinburgh University Press

Fone, Byrne, (2001), *Homophobia: A History*, London, Picador Pan Macmillan

Isay, Richard, (2009), *Being Homosexual: Gay Men and their Development*, New York, Vintage Books

Johnson, Paul and Vanderbeck, Robert M., (2014), *Law Religion and Homosexuality*, Abingdon, Routledge

Katz, Jonathan Ned, (2007/2), *The Invention of Heterosexuality*, Chicago, University of Chicago Press

Muehlenberg, Bill, (2011), *Strained Relations: The Challenge of Homosexuality*, Melbourne, Freedom Publishing

Rasmussen, Mary Lou, (2015), *Progressive Sexuality Education: The Conceits of Secularism*, Abingdon, Routledge

Rosik, Christopher H., (January 2013), 'When Therapists do not acknowledge their Moral Values: Green's Case as a Case Study' in *Journal of Marital and Family Therapy*, Vol. 29, 1, 41

Rosik, Christopher H., (2012), 'Opposite-Gender Identity States in Dissociative Identity Disorder: Psychodynamic Insights into a Subset of Same-Sex Behaviour and Attractions' in *Journal of Psychology and Christianity*, Vol. 31, 3, 2012, pp. 269-275

Satinover, Jeffrey, (1996), *Homosexuality and the Politics of Truth*, Grand Rapids, Baker Books

Weiss, Meredith L. and Bosia, Michael J., (2013), *Global Homophobia: States, Movements and the Politics of Oppression*, Chicago, University of Illinois Press

CHAPTER 9

From Abuse to Proper Use

'"There's glory for you!" "I don't know what you mean by 'glory,'" Alice said. "I meant, 'there's a nice knock-down argument for you!'" "But 'glory' doesn't mean 'a nice knock-down argument,'" Alice objected. "When I use a word," Humpty Dumpty said in a rather scornful tone, "it means just what I choose it to mean – neither more nor less."' (Lewis Carroll, *Alice Through the Looking-Glass*, chapter 7)

By an intriguing coincidence, I have started to write this final summary and review of the abuse of language the day after over 4 million people were reported to have taken to the streets in cities across France to protest in favour of freedom of speech against fanatical groups who seek to patrol thought by means of violent intimidation. Many times, the catch-phrase, "no one has the right not to be offended," has been repeated in defence of coarse and disparaging cartoons aimed at mocking social customs, political ideas and policies and religious beliefs and activities.

I am also a firm advocate of the importance of people being allowed to express, publicly, their innermost convictions without fear of censorship, either by the statute book or random pressure groups. However, I do detect not a little whiff of hypocrisy in the concerted outcry of indignation that followed the horrendous killing of journalists in their own offices as they carried out their trade.

Freedom of expression, belief and conscience is not an absolute right without any restrictions. There are justifiable laws against defamation of character, deliberate misrepresentation of people's views and actions and invasion of privacy. In the case of the French satirical magazine, it could well be argued that some of the portrayals amounted to an abuse of freedom, in that the intended message was designed to be gratuitously offensive by being aggressively mocking and insulting. In the name of freedom, the journalists, in this particular case, abandoned good taste in a kind of anarchic free-for-all. So, the marches and vigils, whilst fully understandable in the face of an unspeakable atrocity, by using the rhetorical excuse of freedom to offend, were in danger of abusing the language of freedom.

As argued in the chapter on freedom, neither the concept nor the reality are first order moral goods. It is not a moral absolute that has to be conceded in every circumstance. Although, as an ideal, it must be guarded carefully against unwarranted restrictions, whether these are officially promulgated through legislation, state intimidation, the pressure of public campaigning, prejudice or ridicule, it does not necessarily trump other unconditional moral virtues. In recent instances of openly proclaimed disagreement with the notion of gay marriage, some authorities have sought to silence those in their employment who have expressed objections, by forbidding them from expressing their views on pain of dismissal from their jobs. This is an unjustifiable assault on free speech. When such people are also accused of being homophobic, intolerant, blinkered and, worst of all, bigoted, those are classic examples of using abusive language.

Some people have argued that freedom of religion, signifying not only freedom to hold and openly champion religious beliefs, but also freedom to act in accordance with those beliefs, is inviolable. So, discrimination against religious believers on the grounds of what they say or do is the equivalent of discrimination against women or racial groups because, without their consent, that is the way they were born. This particular argument is quite clearly wrong, for belief is a matter of choice; gender and ethnic origin is circumstantial.

Nations that aspire to being model, secular democracies must be careful not to restrict the right of religious believers to express their beliefs individually or collectively as they wish. In particular, administrators of the law are not, as such, in a position to interpret the significance of symbolic expressions of belief. However, these rights are not unconditional. Clearly, no nation can allow religious adherents to promote their religion through violent means. The use of any form of coercion, in which people are forced into joining or remaining in a religious group through threat, deception or bribery, falls foul of a justifiable religious freedom, because coercion of any kind is an abuse of freedom.

Other instances of the abuse of language that we have been exploring – for example, the way in which issues of tolerance, equality and rights are often spoken about – as in the case of freedom, do not constitute basic human values. In order to combat the allure of the pseudo-religious propaganda of Islamist groups, committed to violent acts of terror, there is much talk of the need to instil, in young children, the core values of a liberal democracy. In some countries, this is being made a mandatory part of a core curriculum. Such a proposal sounds a most worthy goal. However, there are problems. The most obvious concerns the question of what is defined as a core value. As we have seen clearly, none of the usual candidates for inclusion are wholly self-explanatory and unambiguous.

The original understanding of tolerance, for example, has been reinvented, in recent times, to reflect a cultural change of mood. It often means little more than to accept and condone whatever it is that the person advocating tolerance deems a worthy belief or cause. Intolerance, on the other hand, is usually accorded a blanket, knee-jerk condemnation, even though one can think of many occurrences where intolerance is the right attitude to adopt: for example, towards pornographic literature showing the sexual abuse of young children; incitement to hatred and violence against people who hold views different from one's own; fraud; perjury; false-accusation; deceit; theft; bullying; exploitation, and many more. To tolerate any of these actions would be wholly wrong. By and large, societies have come to accept, in certain cases, the policy of zero tolerance against anti-social behaviour. An automatic negative reaction against the very use of the word intolerance is, therefore, a sign of careless thought.

To advocate equality is, as a general principle, a thoroughly admirable ideal. However, for the sake of an accurate understanding, its meaning and implementation, according to particular circumstances, need to be carefully considered. One of the, perhaps surprising, findings of this survey of the use and abuse of language is to discover how interlocked each concept is. Thus, in order to protect and advance equality strategies, other important values, such as freedom, justice and rights, may well be suppressed. Likewise, issues of equality may be rightly challenged in order to support the values of freedom, tolerance, justice and reasonable accommodation in the case of differing views on what equality entails.

The point about core moral values is that the intrinsic meaning and application of each must be seen in the context of all the others. All must be placed within the frame of reference of what constitutes the two highest virtues of all: absolute truth and the ultimate good. The answer to this question depends on people's world-view: the primary intellectual basis which shapes their convictions about the meaning and purpose of life, the origin and nature of human existence, the cause of and solution to evil, beliefs about the end of life in this world and whether there is any existence after death.

In a pluralist society, such as exists in most nations of the world (even where minority opinions are suppressed by dictatorial regimes), in the nature of the case there will be no agreement on an ultimate and absolute reference point for deciding on what is true and good. World-views, whether founded on religious beliefs, political ideologies or secular principles, are often manifestly conflicting. Thus, arrival at a consensus on what constitutes absolute truth and the ultimate good becomes impossible to achieve. Without a sufficiently well-grounded explanation of how one may know what is true and arrive at the good, the notion of human rights, for example, becomes problematic. Ultimately, the essence of both virtues depends on a convincing theory about what makes human beings human.[86]

In light of the clash of fundamental world-views, to speak conclusively of core values is highly questionable. To trot out the usual menu of worthy ideals, without considering carefully why, and in what way, they are derived from a coherent, consistent and well-founded concept of truth and the good, is to deal in trivia and to promote confusion. Unfortunately, this is precisely what the present proposal achieves. To add to the notion of core values, the phrase "of a liberal democracy" highlights the confusion, since the precise meaning of both liberal and democracy are strongly contested.

Already one can see how the actual implementation of so-called core values is being denied in practice. In the case of such ancient and well-tried institutions as heterosexual marriage and a family, constituted by a mother, father and children, it is apparently wrong to insist that these arrangements in themselves contribute to the good of society. Those who wish to uphold them and to denounce alternative views and practices are now being censured and disciplined in the name of core values, such as absolute respect for other people's views. One might ask, then, which core values are being talked about? Certainly, they are not the core values of freedom,

---

[86] I have, myself, attempted a critical, historical survey of many understandings of what it means to be human: see *Being Human: An Historical Inquiry into Who We Are*, (2019), Eugene, OR: Wipf and Stock.

tolerance, rights and liberal democracy. So, without a fundamental debate about a much more precise understanding of these values, in light of a comprehensive and comprehensible notion of truth and the good, the present use of this language merely intensifies the hypocritical rhetoric of a particular political and ideological agenda.

This study of words, which frequently crop up in public political debate and legal arguments, is intended to point out their degree of misuse and, in some cases, abuse. Sadly, the present situation is helping to create a divided society, in which intolerance of what were once perfectly normal, acceptable and mainstream views is becoming the norm. This state of affairs could be remedied, if people were to commit themselves to explaining carefully and non-polemically how they are using a particular phrase and their underlying justification for using it as they do. Only in this way will good communication be restored and people, with different opinions on major controversies, be able to converse in a dignified and civil manner. The alternative, tragically, is to use language as Humpty Dumpty claimed to use it, giving it his own private meaning and manipulating it as "a knock-down argument."

Lightning Source UK Ltd.
Milton Keynes UK
UKHW040621050220
358203UK00001B/118